Opera
Guide 32

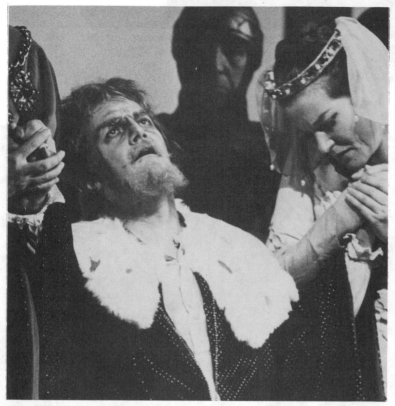

Tito Gobbi as the dying Boccanegra with Orianna Santunione as Amelia, Covent Garden, 1965 (photo: Donald Southern)

Preface

This series, published under the auspices of English National Opera and The Royal Opera, aims to prepare audiences to evaluate and enjoy opera performances. Each book contains the complete text, set out in the original language together with a current performing translation. The accompanying essays have been commissioned as general introductions to aspects of interest in each work. As many illustrations and musical examples as possible have been included because the sound and spectacle of opera are clearly central to any sympathetic appreciation of it. We hope that, as companions to the opera should be, they are well-informed, witty and attractive.

The Royal Opera is most grateful to the The Baring Foundation for sponsoring this Guide.

Nicholas John
Series Editor

32

Simon Boccanegra

Giuseppe Verdi

Opera Guide Series Editor: Nicholas John

*Published in association with
English National Opera and The Royal Opera
and assisted by a generous donation
from The Baring Foundation*

John Calder · London
Riverrun Press · New York

First published in Great Britain, 1985 by
John Calder (Publishers) Ltd.,
18 Brewer Street,
London, W1R 4AS

First published in the U.S.A., 1985 by
Riverrun Press Inc.,
1170 Broadway,
New York, NY 10001

BRITISH LIBRARY CATALOGUING IN PUBLICATION DATA
Verdi, Giuseppe
  Simon Boccanegra. — (Opera guides; 32)
  I. Title   II. Piave, Francesco Maria
  III. Fenton, James   IV. Series
  782.1'2   ML50.V484

LIBARY OF CONGRESS CATALOGING IN PUBLICATION DATA
Verdi, Giuseppe, 1813-1901.
    [Simon Boccanegra. Libretto. English & Italian]
    Simon Boccanegra.

    (Opera Guide; 32)
    Includes libretto by Francesco Maria Piave, rev. by Arrigo Boito, English
translation by James Fenton, and commentary.
    Based on: Simón Boccanegra / Antonio Garcia Gutiérrez.
    Discography: p.
    Bibliography: p.
    1. Operas — Librettos.   2. Verdi, Giuseppe, 1813-1901.
Simon Boccanegra.   I. Piave, Francesco Maria, 1810-1876.
II. Boito, Arrigo, 1842-1918.   III. Fenton, James, 1941-   .   IV. Garcia
Gutiérrez, Antonio, 1813-1884.
Simón Boccanegra.   V. Title   VI. Series.
ML50.V484S52   1985   782.1'092'4   85-1831
ISBN 0-7145-4064-1

SUBSIDISED BY THE
Arts Council
OF GREAT BRITAIN

John Calder (Publishers) Ltd, English National Opera and
The Royal Opera House, Covent Garden Ltd receive
financial assistance from the Arts Council of Great Britain.
English National Opera also receives financial assistance from
the Greater London Council.

Typeset in Plantin by Margaret Spooner Typesetting, Dorchester, Dorset
Printed by the Camelot Press Ltd., Southampton

Contents

List of Illustrations

Picture research: Henrietta Bredin

An Historical Perspective

Rodolfo Celletti

For an opera such as *Simon Boccanegra*, knowledge of the historical background is important. The first version was composed in 1856 and performed in Venice the following year. The unification of Italy had begun but was not yet complete. Verdi's strong views on Italian nationalism are well known and yet the most significant political episode in the opera — the Council scene in Act One — was not incorporated into it until 1881, that is, not until the second version, on which Verdi collaborated with Arrigo Boito. To understand why this was, it is useful to look at the historical events which form the basis of the libretto.

In 1856 Piave took the story of *Simon Boccanegra* from the Spanish Romantic drama of the same name by Antonio Garcia Gutièrrez (who was also the author of the play on which *Il trovatore* had been based four years earlier). But Simon Boccanegra was, of course, a real historical figure in mid-14th century Genoa. Genoa was at that time the bitter rival of Venice for maritime power and their trading interests clashed especially in the Eastern Mediterranean, where the lands of the Byzantine Greek Empire offered enormous potential. The city suffered, as much as other Italian city states, from endemic civil feuds. There was an underlying rivalry between the semi-feudal nobility, the families of Doria, Spinola, Fieschi and Grimaldi, and the non-noble townspeople. In the previous century, with growing sea-power and wealth, the townspeople had developed a form of self-government to counterbalance the autocratic unruliness of the landed nobility. The 'Popolo' elected a council, but the question of who elected the leaders of the council (the two Captains and the Abbot) was disputed between the Popolo and the nobles. Simon Boccanegra's uncle, Guglielmo, was the most famous of the Captains of the People, 1257-1262. The nobles quarreled among themselves, and their rivalries were polarized by the pretensions of Pope and Emperor to the overlordship of Italy. Thus the Doria and Spinola were allied to the Imperial Ghibelline cause, and the Fieschi and Grimaldi supported the Papal Guelphs. Within the city each family cultivated, by networks of intermarriage and obligation, an area where their power was paramount and, in the regular outbreaks of feuding, these areas could be sealed off and effectively used as strongholds. The Popolo were united principally by their desire for stability, although they were just as liable to split into factions as the nobles.

After the death of the Emperor Henry VII in 1313, the nobles profited from the unsettled political situation in Italy to sell their services as professional soldiers. The consequent increase in their power weakened the commune of Genoa with years of savage feuding. Finally, in 1339, the Popolo turned upon the nobles and demanded a leader of their own election; they chose Simon Boccanegra, not as one of two Captains, or as Abbot, but as their first Doge, with the powers, however circumscribed, of a sole leader. He appears to have been reluctant to assume the responsibility, and his first five years in office were marked by wise and sober government. (He was not, as the libretto claims, a pirate; that was his brother, Egidio.) While he reduced the most violent of the nobility to obedience, he saved the life of one of the Grimaldi

7

who was his personal enemy and curbed the extremes of the factions of the Popolo. During his reign the naval importance of the city was maintained with victories against the Turks, the Tartars and the Moors. Nevertheless, the hostility of the combined feudal nobility eventually reasserted itself; he was also opposed by some of the rich merchant class who saw his policies run counter to their own aggrandisement. In 1344 he renounced the Dogeship and withdrew into private life. The office of Doge, however, was retained.

During the next ten years the Genoese campaigns against the Venetians, the Byzantine Greeks and the Turks drained the city's resources. In 1351 Petrarch appealed to Andrea Dandolo, Doge of Venice, invoking Italian fraternity between the two maritime republics. In the following year he addressed a similar letter to the Genoese. But to no effect. A phyrric victory for the Genoese in the Bosphorous was followed by defeat by the Venetian fleet at Lojèra (off Sardinia) in 1353. Genoa appealed to Venice's most powerful enemy on land, Archbishop Giovanni Visconti, lord of Milan and most of Lombardy, for protection. The Venetians refused the overtures of peace, made by the Archbishop and actually presented by Petrarch as ambassador, for fear this would merely give him time to consolidate his power against them in Genoa. In 1354 a Genoese victory over the Venetians at Porto Lungho avenged Lojera. Two years later the Genoese threw off the overlordship of Milan and recalled Boccanegra from retirement in Pisa. During this second term of office he again excited the opposition both of the feudal nobility and the wealthier citizens. Several attemps were made on his life and in 1363 he was fatally poisoned.

So much is history. It is also possible to look further ahead and say that Gabriele Adorno — that is the tenor role in the opera — was elected Doge on the death of Simon. He belonged to one of the wealthy Popolani families, among whom the Dogeship was from then on contested, and was not, as Piave's libretto suggests, a noble. He showed himself weak and irresolute in office and retired in 1370.

Let us now return to 1881 and the final version of the opera. This consists of a prologue followed by three acts, instead of the four acts of the first version. The most important innovation was the introduction of the Council scene which transforms Boccanegra from an anxious father-figure and a merely disappointed Doge into a prophet of Italian unity. It was Verdi's idea in the first place. In 1880 he made up his mind to revise the opera after its virtual disaster twenty-three years earlier. He decided to leave the first and last acts unchanged and to make only a few adjustments to Act Three. It was Act Two that was the stumbling block — it needed more variety and more vitality. In the same year Verdi wrote along these lines to Giulio Ricordi, adding: 'I recall two remarkable letters from Petrarch, one written to Doge Boccanegra,' [Verdi's memory is at fault here as Boccanegra was not Doge in 1352, when Petrarch wrote to the people of Genoa] 'the other to the Doge of Venice telling them that they were about to throw themselves into fratricidal conflict, that both were sons of the same mother, Italy, etc., etc.' (the 'etc.,etc.' are Verdi's own). Verdi continues: 'This feeling for an Italian motherland is quite remarkable for that time! (Sublime questo sentimento d'una patria italiana in quell' epoca!) This is all political, not dramatic, but a skilful hand could certainly dramatise the situation. For example, Boccanegra, with this idea in mind, would follow the poet's advice — convene the Senate or a private Council, meeting and reveal the letter, with its amazing concept, to them. Everyone horrified — haranguing — anger — final accusation against the

8

Set designs by Pietro Bertojo for the 1857 Venice production: The Prologue (above) and Act Two (below) (Royal Opera House Archives)

Doge of treachery, etc., etc.. The wrangling interrupted by the abduction of Amelia . . .'

Up to this point, these were Verdi's own thoughts and this plot — or rather, this treatment of history — was exactly the basis upon which Boito built the Council scene in which Boccanegra, in the name of Petrarch, advocates a reconciliation with Venice. Yet there is another factor in the new characterisation of the Doge.

When Verdi wrote to Giulio Ricordi about Petrarch's letters, Italy had been unified for almost twenty years. It was rather a 'rickety table' — to use an expression with which Verdi and Boito liked to describe *Simon Boccanegra* when revising it — but at least it existed. And the ideals of the Risorgimento were still fresh in the memory, so much so in fact that it seemed miraculous that they had at last been translated into reality. It is easy to imagine how men of culture and patriotism such as Verdi and Boito would react to a historical episode when Italian unity was envisaged, and brotherhood among Italians was invoked: it would be an inspiration to recreate it, to make it live again for their compatriots.

Such an episode was the ephemeral but epic career of Cola di Rienzo, Tribune of the Roman People for seven months in 1347. In Boito's libretto Boccanegra is portrayed with just those characteristics of the Roman Tribune which might be described as Messianic, when he terrifies Paolo into condemning the man who abducted Amelia. In 1343 this low-born notary had journeyed to Avignon from Rome and won the support of Pope Clement VI and of Petrarch with his flamboyant rhetoric and burning denunciation of the quarrels of the Roman nobles which then impoverished the Holy City. When Cola staged his coup d'état in 1347, Petrarch wrote lengthy letters praising his

Gwynne Howell as Fiesco at Covent Garden, 1981, in the production by Filippo Sanjust (photo: Donald Southern)

defence of the ancient liberties of Rome. Indeed Cola immediately and effectively suppressed the over-mighty Roman nobility, and summoned a parliament to enact new laws to deal with poverty and civil disorder, the city administration and the machinery of justice. In a matter of weeks he established an unaccustomed peace and order in the city and its environs. His guiding principle, declared to all, was that the liberation of Rome from the feudal nobility was also the liberation of Italy.

Word quickly spread throughout Italy of these exploits and of what he had achieved in such a short time. He kept the people informed of every step he took, always urging on them the importance of brotherhood between the Italian cities. His envoys visited every region, taking with them a small silver staff as proof of their identity. The people they met on the way were so moved that they knelt before them, asking if they might kiss the token which symbolised for them the idea of unity among the Italians.

Cola did all he could to promote his vision of a national parliament. Ambassadors converged on Rome from all the Italian cities and, as Petrarch wrote, 'Italy rose up as though spellbound and the glory and dread of the name of Rome reached to the far corners of the world.'

He fell victim, however, to the proud and divisive sense of independence among the city states of Italy, as well as to his own mad excesses; in Rome he lost the favour of the Popolo, and even the Orsini and the Colonna set aside their ancient quarrels in order to oust him. Petrarch, who had set out from Avignon to offer his advice to the Tribune, had reached Genoa by November 1347 when he received news of Cola's immoderate behaviour:

> Shall the world then see you fall from the leader of the good to become the partner of the vile? . . . I cannot alter matters, but I can flee them.

A determined uprising of the nobles on December 15 was hardly resisted by Cola's militia, and he fled to Naples. After several years in secure but comfortable prisons in Germany and Avignon, he returned as a puppet of the Papacy to rule Rome a second time in 1353. He once again lost the support of the people and was killed by the mob.

The Council scene in the 1881 *Simon Boccanegra* captures the upsurge of Italian national feeling which Petrarch encouraged with such spectacular, if short-lived, success in Cola di Rienzo's Rome. It captures the highly charged political atmosphere of 14th-century Italy and recalls the passionate arguments of Dante's *De Monarchia* (1313), pleading for a strong leader to deliver Italy from present turmoil, and the apocalyptic visions of Joachim of Flora, predicting that the Anti-Christ's reign would precede the Last Judgement. For men of the Risorgimento like Verdi and Boito, it was an epoch which naturally carried extraordinary poetic resonance. Simone's climactic peroration ('All that I ask is peace, now! All that I ask is love!') is not an expression of the historical Simone's love for his city but of the visions of Cola di Rienzo, of Dante and of Petrarch, of Verdi and Boito themselves — indeed of all those who had dreamt over the centuries of unity, peace and brotherhood among the people of Italy.

The whole of Boccanegra's peroration is in fact worth attention: even as he appeals for peace the opposing factions of the Genoese come to blows. For there is one further point to be noticed: when Verdi composed *The Sicilian Vespers* in 1855 he had written his last opera with a patriotic *risorgimentale* theme. All the subsequent works (the first version of *Simon Boccanegra*, *A Masked Ball*, *The Force of Destiny*, *Don Carlos*, *Aida*) carry the marks of the

11

Kiri te Kanawa as Amelia and Boris Christoff as Fiesco at Covent Garden in 1973 (photo: Donald Southern)

new Italian situation: the unification of Italy about to be completed (*Boccanegra* in 1857) or actually completed. Verdi, as poet of the Risorgimento, as the musical voice of an oppressed people, stood to one side and was silent: his job was done. But the Council scene of the 1881 *Simon Boccanegra* rekindled his old political passion. And so *Simon Boccanegra* is important because, for the last time, Verdi, one of the central characters in the new movement for unity within the young state, returned to the theme that he had so passionately supported in earlier years. He was then 68 years old, and perhaps disillusioned and embittered by the events following unification, but his voice still comes across firm and fervent, as he recalls the old ideals of the heroic years of the Risorgimento.

An Introduction to the 1881 Score

James A. Hepokoski

Although undeniably a masterpiece, *Simon Boccanegra* presents us with complexities that, while by no means insurmountable, are not easily resolved. As audiences soon discover, the libretto is strained and problematic — a patchwork text produced by no fewer than three hands. And, as an opera that Verdi revised long after its first performance, *Simon Boccanegra* is a conflation of two separate musical visions, not a single, spontaneous unity. The original version of the opera was first performed (unsuccessfully) at Venice's La Fenice on March 12, 1857; the rather thorough overhauling of the work, whose extraordinary new music foreshadows the later *Otello*, was first given at La Scala on March 24, 1881. We are thus invited to absorb a stylistically checkered work, which juxtaposes two successful, but sharply contrasting, styles. The danger here, of course, is that of fragmentation, the division of the opera into separate, mutually exclusive moments.

Verdi wrote the 1857 *Simon Boccanegra* during a period of emerging experimentation, stylistic growth, and expansion. On the one hand it resounded with clear echoes of his earlier style. The basic musical conventions of the *Risorgimento* (separate numbers with breaks for applause, multi-movement arias and duets with repetitive codas, cadenzas, and repeated cabalettas, static *concertato* ensembles, and so on) were indeed present, if usually modified — sometimes in ways that seemed to mystify his contemporaries; the musical discourse was characteristically terse, angular, and muscular — often a succession of short, sharp blows or rising groundswells; the accompaniment patterns, although more ingenious, often still relied on pulsating, repetitive rhythms to generate their energy; and much of the orchestration perpetuated the simpler Italian tradition. On the other hand, the original *Simon Boccanegra* contained a number of 'progressive' (but not revolutionary) elements. Some of these are traceable to Verdi's growing knowledge of French grand opera (his last complete work had been *Les vêpres siciliennes* for Paris in 1855). Others stemmed from his increasing willingness to subordinate lyricism as an end in itself to the interests of general mood, dramatic flow, and character depiction and to heighten the dramatically active, non-formal sections — everything, that is, that surrounds the more static, lyrical pieces. But to many of Verdi's contemporaries this suggested a dangerous tilt away from Italianate melodic supremacy. The most famous remarks are those of the Florentine Abramo Basevi in 1859:

> With this opera Verdi attempted a *fourth manner*, almost approaching Germanic music through its affected use of new forms to be adapted to the dramatic expression, its greater importance given to the recitatives, and its lesser concern about melody. I would almost say, to judge at least from the Prologue, that he wanted to follow (albeit at a distance) the footsteps of the famous Wagner, the subverter of present-day music. It is well known that Wagner would like to make music as determined a language as possible, almost the shadow of the poetry.

This 'non-lyrical' impression, particularly when coupled with the complicated

13

libretto, made *Simon Boccanegra* a 'difficult' work for 1857, and the opera failed to find a secure place in the repertoire. In the ensuing fourteen years it was mounted only some three dozen times, mostly in provincial theatres, with varying success. Its last production in a major theatre was at the Teatro Regio in Turin in 1864; its last gasp in Verdi's lifetime was a production in Trani in 1871.

Verdi's revision of the music in January and February 1881 (a kind of pre-*Otello* project) went hand in hand with a simultaneous revision of the text by the gifted Arrigo Boito — a revision that went so far as to produce an entirely new scene: Act One, scene two, the Council Chamber scene. (Julian Budden provides the details of this collaboration in his masterly study, *The Operas of Verdi*.) Clearly, the most dated music had to be excised or rewritten, the original breaks smoothed over with transitions, and the like, but Verdi's alterations went far beyond the minimum requirements. Nearly every piece was affected in some way — some entire sections recomposed, elsewhere a bass line altered here, a vocal phrase there, and so on. The principal passages of 1881 music (many of which were based on thematic and harmonic material from the corresponding passages of the 1857 version) are indicated in the discussion further below.

Verdi's revision of *Simon Boccanegra* merits attention as the threshold of his late style: the gateway that leads to a rich outpouring (including the 1882-83 *Don Carlos* revisions, *Otello*, *Falstaff*, and the *Four Sacred Pieces*) that remains one of the glories of nineteenth-century music. By 1881 he had deepened nearly every aspect of his music in intensity, motivic coherence, and variety of colour. His task in revising *Simon Boccanegra* amounted to recasting a work conceived in one aesthetic value-system (the 'old world' of the *Risorgimento*) according to the demands of another, more 'modern' one. Particularly noticeable is the increased sophistication and activity of the orchestra. In Verdi's late style the orchestra is frequently the bearer of developing motivic fragments that bind the larger sections of the work together. These motifs are continually being reshaped and varied; the composer seems to have come to consider literal repetition an aesthetic error, and scarcely any 1881 idea appears the same way twice. The reigning principle is that of spontaneous 'organic' growth. A hard-won mastery of this new organic style (one progressively defined in *Un ballo in maschera*, *La forza del destino*, *Don Carlos*, *Aida* and the *Messa da Requiem*) permitted Verdi to conceive music more flexibly and broadly, over longer stretches of time, than in 1857. This was precisely the remedy to bring to the earlier *Simon Boccanegra*. Moreover, by 1881 Verdi had also constructed a new lyricism, one that rounded the sharp edges of his earlier, Italian melodic style with the supple contours and ripe sensuousness of France, all underscored with a luscious *chiaroscuro* chromatic harmony. The practical effect of all of this in the revised opera is dramatic and palpable. At critical moments the characters break out of their 1857 limitations and into a more freely flowing, rapturous lyricism. This is the invasion of one world by another, the sudden breach of a ritualistic, honour-bound society with surges of 'natural feeling'. It is true that the danger for any apprehension of *Simon Boccanegra* as an aesthetic whole is that the richer, later music can diminish the effect of the earlier. But the very disparity of musical styles can function dramatically, particularly when one accepts the 1857 style as normative and prevailing, the ground for more 'spontaneous' excursions into heightened individual feeling.

Prologue

The opening scenes of *Simon Boccanegra* begin in Verdi's purest 1881 manner and gradually drift back to his 1857 style. His mature present, that is, is called upon to conjure up the past, a procedure not unlike that of storytelling. Accordingly, the opera is launched in a relaxed, rocking, 'once-upon-a-time' vein — unique in Verdi's mature operas (and a radical change from the original, tense 1857 Prelude). The first scene, with Pietro and Paolo's plotting and Simone's ultimate acceptance of the offer to become Doge, centres around the opening theme [1], which, bobbing gently on sea-deep string harmonies, also suggests something of the marine atmosphere that will pervade so much of this opera. As is typical of late Verdi, this central theme is continually developed ('organically') and varied, moves into dialogue with interruptions and interpolations (some recalling 1857 music), and is

Tito Gobbi as the young Simon Boccanegra in the Prologue of his own production at Covent Garden in 1965 (photo: Reg Wilson)

fragmented and reshaped according to the demands of the drama. With Simone's exit and Paolo's withdrawal to one side, a new section of nocturnal music begins [2]. Hushed, delicately scored, and conspiratorial (and foreshadowing the conclusion of Act Three, scene one of *Falstaff*), these night whispers are shaped in much the same way as was the preceding section: an initial orchestral statement (for the entrance of Pietro and the sailors and workers) is repeated — and varied, developed, and interrupted — with dialogue. The chorus's surprise at Paolo's abrupt proposal of 'Simone Boccanegra' as the next Doge is one of the celebrated features of the 1881 score: a sudden, *forte* shout, 'Simone!', gives way to a stunned, quizzical 'Il Corsaro!', sung *sotto voce*.

With Paolo's E-minor *racconto* [3], the Prologue settles largely into 1857 music (although the original was up a step, in F-sharp minor). The squarer melodic cut, the pungently reedy woodwind doubling, and the propulsive drive of Verdi's earlier style are instantly perceptible. Still, for 1857, this was an advanced piece, both harmonically and structurally. It is built from two long musical strophes, the second freely varying the first (notice, for instance, its more active accompaniment). Each strophe begins with Paolo alone and warms up into a choral response. The second strophe's response, however, includes dialogue between Paolo and the chorus — an embedding of more ongoing drama into a 'formal' strophe. Verdi lightly touched up the piece's orchestration and accompaniment in 1881, and one passage is new: the *dolcissimo* conclusion of the first strophe, 'Passando ogni pietoso' [4] — a sudden, warm glow, again with *marinesco* flavouring. The orchestral 'exit-music', with its eerily gleaming high open-fifths, is an expansion of the original conclusion.

Despite its smooth accompaniment and evocative use of offstage chorus, Fiesco's bass *romanza*, 'Il lacerato spirito' [5], is the most traditional piece of the 1857 Prologue. Its antique feel (a reworking of the minor-major formula, with the usual formal, repeated coda lines) and deep severity of tone perfectly capture Fiesco's 'old-world' nobility. This is, after all, the first appearance of a proud Guelph, whose very life upholds ritualized patterns of honour and social status. An even more intensified ceremonial quality may be felt in the double-groundswell orchestral postlude (1857) as the mourners leave Fiesco's palace.

The bitter Simone-Fiesco duet that follows, however, violates the conventional expectations of 1857 and is a landmark of Verdi's maturing style. The traditional duet-pattern found so often in his earlier operas passed through five phases: an introductory *scena* (recitative-setting of unrhymed verse); a *tempo d'attacco* (dramatically active dialogue, typically without repeated lines and often set in *parlante* style, that is, with the principal melody in the orchestra — specifically, this movement begins with the onset of rhymed, regular verse and almost always signifies a sudden gain in dramatically shaped, directional energy); a break in the forward motion for the lyrical *adagio* (formal, static stanzas with coda — *adagio* here is a formal term, not a description of the tempo actually indicated); a *tempo di mezzo* (active connecting movement); and a brilliant, rousing *cabaletta* (like the *adagio*, formal stanzas, but characteristically featuring a large-scale musical and textual repetition before the coda proper). But this baritone-bass duet (small portions of which were retouched in 1881) becomes more structurally ambiguous as it proceeds. There are no truly 'static' sections in the traditional sense, and the text lacks formal *cabaletta* stanzas. The aesthetic point is clear:

16

the rapid current of the dramatic action is reluctant to relax into lyrical pools. The *tempo d'attacco* blazes forth (with a few 1881 retouchings) at Fiesco's 'Qual cieco fato' [6], but the argument burns on much longer than anticipated in juxtaposed, contrasting musical sections. Fiesco's *meno mosso* appeal for his grandchild, 'Se concedermi vorrai', may at first seem to begin a formal *adagio*, but this impression soon vanishes. The actual *adagio*, or *adagio* substitute, is Simone's *racconto*, 'Del mar sul lido' [7], with its salt-water tang (notice the 'sea-breeze' woodwind doubling). The decisive structural and dramatic point here is its breaking of the continuity of present time through a flashback into the past, not so much its internal structure: ultimately, the piece dissolves into dialogue. The whole duet up to the point of Fiesco's low-F 'Addio' is constructed of instantaneous music that parallels the unfolding drama. It is one of the most advanced structures of the original *Simon Boccanegra* — and one that drew especially heavy fire from Basevi, who considered the duet to have ended with the *racconto*. The Prologue concludes as in 1857: a dramatic *'scena'* (actually functioning as an appended *tempo di mezzo* and thus in some senses continuing the duet), as Simone discovers the dead Maria, leads to the final chorus (a dramatic substitute for a conventional *cabaletta*). Here the people unknowingly mock Simone's grief and goad Fiesco to even further wrath by hailing the corsair as Doge to the accompaniment of vigorous (and, for Verdi, purposely trivial) *Risorgimento* 'public-music' — very much in the old style.

Act One

Scene One. A new, closed-curtain prelude (based on some of the 1857 material) presents us with one of the jewels of the 1881 score: an evocative tone-picture of dawn by the sea, graced with airy violin trills and tremolos, broad viola waves, and gentle woodwind bubbling. With the rise of the curtain onto the coastal garden of the Grimaldi palace — now twenty-five years later than the Prologue — Amelia begins her *cavatina* [8]. The French-influenced, ABA[1] melody is mostly from 1857, but the sophisticated accompaniment — more bubbling woodwind — is new. True to his 1881 principle of non-repetition, Verdi provides a different accompaniment for the musical reprise ('O altero ostel'). And entirely new to 1881 is Amelia's exquisite conclusion, 'S'inalba il ciel', which rises up to a delicious, *dolcissimo* high B-flat and rounds with the woodwind bubbling and string tremolos of the prelude: everything heard thus far has been, as Verdi put it, 'a unified piece'.

In 1857 Amelia followed Gabriele's Manrico-like offstage song [9] with a solo *cabaletta*, but in the revision we plunge at once (after some skilful 1881 stitching, 'Ei vien!' etc.) into the first of the three duets of Act One, scene one, the 'Duetto Amelia e Gabriele', mostly from 1857. The two lovers pass through the *scena* — Amelia reveals her knowledge of Gabriele's rebellious plotting with the other Guelphs — directly into the *adagio*, 'Vieni a mirar la cerula'. (In sharp contrast with the duet in the Prologue Verdi chooses not to include a *tempo d'attacco*. Here the dramatic point, one supposes, is either that it has been 'hushed away' by Gabriele or that Amelia's concern pushes her prematurely into her formal plea.) Amelia begins her melody by floating a perfectly still D natural (of which Basevi did not approve) on top of soft, wave-like string lappings and woodwind trills, then, more purposefully, expands into the broad, coquettishly tempting refrain [10], which Gabriele also shares at the end of his 1881-enriched *risposta*, or formal response. A rapid, recitative-like

17

Act One, scene six (above) and the Council Chamber scene (below) from the production at La Scala, Milan, by Giorgio Strehler, designed by Ezio Frigerio, which toured to Covent Garden in 1976 (photos: Ezio Piccagliani)

18

tempo di mezzo in which Pietro announces the Doge's imminent arrival (and we learn that Paolo hopes to marry Amelia) obliges the lovers to bring the duet to a hasty close with a shortened *cabaletta* [11], also retouched in 1881.

The Gabriele/Fiesco duet that follows underwent a heavier revision. Fiesco, our severe noble, begins his *scena* account of Amelia's humble origins in smooth 1881 recitative ('Alto mistero'). His more prosaic telling-of-the-tale ('No, — la figlia dei Grimaldi') remains in an aged and bone-weary 1857 *arioso*. But when Gabriele re-declares his love for Amelia ('L'orfana adoro') the music swims wondrously into the wide-eyed richness of 1881. It is one of the most moving moments of the revised opera: the stiff, deep-bass Fiesco thaws in the warmth of more spontaneous, quasi-religious emotion. Even more striking than the C-major paternal blessing [12] (structurally considered, the onset of a compact *adagio*) is Gabriele's juxtaposed E-minor *risposta* [13], wafting ecstatically heavenward and climaxing with a 'sacred' pseudo-modal lift in the accompaniment as he reaches the peak of his vocal line (on the word 'voce').

The ensuing duet between Amelia and Simone likewise mixes the 1857 and 1881 styles, but is more traditionally shaped: it is the first duet to pass through all of the five conventional duet-phases. In the *scena*, beginning immediately after the offstage trumpet fanfares announce the Doge's arrival, Fiesco and Gabriele withdraw, savouring the Guelph rebellion to come (the 1857 version had contained a much longer *giuramento*, or oath, between the two), Paolo gloats briefly over Amelia, and Simone pardons Amelia's exiled brothers — all to an 1881 recitative with carefully nuanced orchestral interjections. The *tempo d'attacco* [14] begins in Verdi's typically middle-period 'conversation-style', a relaxed *parlante* (whose rhythms, at least, recall the much slower, more grotesque Rigoletto/ Sparafucile encounter), gaining in intensity and finally growing into the 1881 style for her dramatic revelation to Simone that she is not really a Grimaldi by birth. The largely 1857 *adagio* [15] resonates with a timbre and mood heard often in Verdi: a woodwind introduction — here an oboe, but in 1857 the scoring may have called for a clarinet — leads the way into a melancholy soprano solo. This *adagio*, once again, is not the traditional static reflection. It is another flexible, prolonged *racconto*, moving and changing along with the dramatic information that it contains — a bold procedure for 1857. It grows out of its initial G minor into G major ('Mi baciò' — the expected musical reprise is replaced by an entirely new melody), elicits a brief, hopeful *risposta* from Simone, who now suspects that she might be his long-lost daughter, and surges into rapturous 1881 lyricism in the coda, as Amelia and Simone sing simultaneously [16]. The *tempo di mezzo* brings back the rhythms of the 'conversational' *parlante* heard earlier [14] — the climactic 'Ah! stringi al sen Maria che t'ama' is from 1881, but most of the succeeding orchestral outburst was present in the early score — and leads to the *cabaletta* [17], an 1857 piece thoroughly reworked in 1881 (or, better, an 1881 composition with a good memory for its 1857 predecessor). Particularly invigorating is Amelia's *risposta* [18], impulsively springing forth and arching broadly over a wide range in the *Aida* style: in the 1857 score she had dutifully repeated her father's melody (even retaining its throbbing-pulse accompaniment). At the close of the coda father and daughter embrace to a beatified restatement of [17] (notice

19

*Sherrill Milnes as Boccanegra and Leona Mitchell as Amelia, Covent Garden, 1981
(photo: Donald Southern)*

the 'celestial' harp — *musica angelica*). After such a lyrically effusive duet,
Simone's denial of Amelia to Paolo and Paolo's and Pietro's terse *parlante*
plans to kidnap Amelia, although dramatically necessary, inevitably seem
a letdown.

Scene Two. The 1881 Council Chamber Scene, the high point of the
revised score, is a highly complex and fluid structure. It may be grasped,
however, by realizing that it rests on three central musical blocks: the
insurrection, Amelia's recounting of her abduction, and the climactic
appeal for peace. Each block is preceded by introductory or transition
material. After a rancorous and confrontational orchestral introduction
that gets nowhere [19], giving us some idea of the deep-seated conflicts
within the group that Simone is addressing, three swelling string chords —
the depth of Verdi's new mastery of harmonic colour is felt at once — lead
to Simone's initial requests for peace (one a message from Petrarch).
Agitated refusals within the chamber give way to the muffled sounds of a
rebellion outside. The insurrection motif [20a], strangely reminiscent of
the second movement of Beethoven's Quartet, Op. 130, dominates the first
large block of music — quintessentially late Verdi. The four-measure
motif appears no fewer than eleven times in *crescendo* — a mounting
whirlwind of varied settings through differing keys and textures,
interrupted briefly by scattered episodic material. The music rushes
towards two climactic statements: the C minor quasi-reprise, 'Armi,
saccheggio' [20b] and (following a wonderful 'spatial' effect as the
trumpet-call in the orchestra passes to the offstage trumpet and the
immediate threat to the Doge is quelled) the E-minor *fortissimo* orchestral
explosion ('Ecco le plebi!') as Gabriele, Fiesco, and the crowd burst into
the chamber.

The Council Chamber scene in Tito Gobbi's production, designed by Giancarlo Bartolini Salimbeni at Covent Garden, 1965 (photo: Houston Rogers, Theatre Museum)

Freer, dramatic transitional material for the Simone-Gabriele confrontation and the sudden appearance of Amelia leads to the second, smaller block: her narrative of her abduction [21], the first portion of which is based on 1857 material. Its rounded, but freely organic construction, however, is distinctly in the later style: notice, for instance, the radically varied reprise, in the strings only, beginning two measures before her words, 'Confuso di tema'. Another strife-torn transition (Amelia having claimed knowledge of who originated the plot, the rival factions begin again to accuse each other) brings us to the third block of the scene. This *pezzo concertato* begins with Simone's desperate appeals to end the dissension [22]: it is Verdi's political credo as well, underpinned by an ardent faith in a unified, healed *patria*. Every line is carefully and rhetorically nuanced ('Patrizi!' is set higher than 'Plebe!'; the unifying concept, 'Popolo', highest of all, etc.), and the whole grows from stern reprimands to warm evocations of the soil itself ('Piango su voi!') and climaxes in the most memorable lines of this scene, perhaps of the opera: a quotation from Petrarch [23], who by this point in the scene has been elevated to a quasi-mystical symbol of Italian unity. The *concertato* proper that follows is one of Verdi's most effective and is built around Fiesco's factional laments, Amelia's sweepingly beautiful, personal appeal to Fiesco [24], and Simone's more generalized repetition of the Petrarch quotation [23]. After the close of the *concertato* (i.e., in a *tempo di mezzo* without *stretta*) all eyes turn penetratingly onto the treacherous Paolo, and the music (beginning with a *tutta forza*, almost 'Brucknerian' orchestral unison) resounds with Iago-like ferocity in its twisted shape and nasty trilling [25]. A dry, bass-clarinet solo, a writhing minor-key compression of [24], underscores the Doge's suspicions. As Simone forces Paolo to lay a curse upon his own head [26], the bass clarinet, almost

21

inaudibly, begins to groan repeatedly downward in three descending half-steps. In the next act Paolo will turn this motif into a symbol of deadly revenge.

Act Two

After a few 1857 words between Pietro and Paolo, the former leaves and the latter gives vent to a venomous dramatic *scena* from 1881; one of Boito's and Verdi's many deepenings of the character of Paolo in the revised score. Like Rigoletto's much earlier 'Pari siamo' (except now in cleverly rhyming poetry) this monologue consists of enhanced recitative delivered as dramatically as possible. In this instance its binding forces are fearful echoes of the preceding scene [26]: Simone's curse, rising thrice like searing apparitions in the trumpets and trombones, and the groaning, three-note chromatic descent of Paolo's self-curse, which now becomes the Poison Motif of his assassination plot.

Another largely 1857 'conversational' *parlante*, this time with Paolo attempting unsuccessfully to tempt the ever-proud Fiesco into murdering the Doge in his sleep [27] — a boldly separate musical structure (like that of the Rigoletto-Sparafucile dialogue), unattached in any conventional way to a larger, more predictable unit — brings us to a similarly early *scena ed aria* for Gabriele. Here again the 1857 Verdi has defied the expected conventions, this time by reversing the positions of the two formal portions of the standard aria structure. And the innovation, as always, matches and articulates the flow of the drama. Incited by Paolo's insinuations that Amelia may have already fallen victim to the Doge's love, Gabriele (of course unaware that the two are father and daughter) assumes the worst and plunges into plans for revenge: a premature, truncated *cabaletta*-howl [28], raging over furiously rushing, chromatic strings (which had already threatened to erupt in the *scena*). Only after Gabriele's thoughts turn fearfully to the possibility of Amelia's deflowering does he soften into a more conventional *adagio* [29] with coda and cadenza (the most old-fashioned solo of the opera). Suddenly Amelia herself appears and a new formal duet is launched directly with the *tempo d'attacco* (emotions are running too high for a mere *scena*), which proceeds breathlessly with Gabriele's tormented fears and accusations and concludes with Amelia's pronouncement (rewritten in 1881) that the reason for her love of Simone must temporarily remain a secret. The *adagio* that follows [30], Gabriele (over an anguished-heartbeat string accompaniment) begging her to reveal the secret and Amelia trying gently to reassure him, is pure 1857 Verdi: two three-phrase melodies, each climaxing on their third phrase. The coda, as their voices join, suddenly 'elevates' for eight measures in the luscious 1881 style. As was the case with their earlier duet in Act One, this duet is cut short by the prospect of Simone's imminent arrival. Accordingly, the *tempo di mezzo* and *cabaletta*-substitute ('All'ora istessa'), both products of 1857, are again telescoped and quickly disposed of: the still-distraught Gabriele vows to assassinate the Doge — his presumed rival — and Amelia hides her furious lover on the balcony before her father arrives.

Everything that follows in Act Two is conceived as a single unit: a finale in 1857 style, retouched here and there in 1881. The culmination of the extraordinarily lengthy *scena* is Simone's soliloquy and inadvertent self-poisoning: the insertion of a semi-formal monologue into a section of

Ingvar Wixell as Boccanegra and Ruggero Raimondi as Fiesco, Covent Garden, 1972 (photo: Donald Southern)

heightened recitative. Verdi revised its opening in 1881 (the bass-pizzicato music immediately surrounding the Doge's sipping of the poison), but with the onset of the light staccato strings the music is from 1857. Simone nods asleep — the staccato string figures yawn further apart — and begins to dream, deeply troubled by what he has just learned: that his daughter (symbolized by the recall of the theme of their recognition *cabaletta* [17] in the woodwind) loves Gabriele, his enemy and fierce partisan of the rebellious Guelphs. After Gabriele emerges to murder the sleeping Doge, the music follows a more predictable course. With Amelia's sudden interposition the *tempo d'attacco* shoots forth [31], tumbling forward to orchestral hammerblows as Simone calls upon Gabriele to strike with his dagger, and concluding in a march-like passage for Simone that contains — finally — the stunning revelation that he is Amelia's father. The *terzetto* that follows (the static, formal movement, heavily retouched in 1881) is one of Verdi's most beautiful short ensembles [32]. Surely no finer example of close psychological depiction can be found than that in Gabriele's opening solo exposition. It consists of three contrasting phrases. In the first he begs Amelia's pardon in E-flat minor. He then turns nobly to the Doge in an open, hand-on-heart passage in the relative G-flat major, admits his assassination plot, and shifts to an anguished third phrase (intensified in 1881) [33] whose end ('il ciglio a te non oso alzar') perfectly traces the course of his shame-filled eyes. The 1857 offstage Guelph chorus that concludes the act [34] functions as the *stretta* (rapid conclusion) of the ensemble. In its muscular, clipped vigour it is a typical *Risorgimento* product (like the concluding chorus in the Prologue). In 1881 Verdi did, however, add women's voices and rewrite the onstage switching of Gabriele's loyalties to the forces of the Doge.

Act Three

Another closed-curtain prelude (from 1881: notice the racing bass line) brings back the vigorous Guelph-rebellion music with which the last act ended [34]. From behind the curtain cries of victory for the Doge overturn the nobles' musical forces, and, by curtain-rise, the initial A-flat minor has brightened into A-flat major. Inside the Doge's palace the captain of Simone's crossbowmen releases Fiesco, restores his sword, and informs him of the Guelph defeat. At this point Fiesco sees the traitor Paolo being led to execution. Paolo's 1881 music here, parallel to his dramatic *scena* at the opening of Act Two (and as Iago-like as ever), is organised around a *forte*, serpentine motif [35] heard at its beginning and end, varied restatements of the Poison Motif [26] as he reveals to Fiesco that Boccanegra is doomed, and his free, jealous remarks (including his admission that it was he who abducted Amelia) as he hears Amelia's and Gabriele's serene, offstage (1857) wedding chorus. After Paolo is led off, Fiesco, although Simone's bitter enemy, shudders (with tremolo strings) at the horror of the poisoning and withdraws into the shadows to await the stricken Doge, who is still unaware of his fate. The Doge's captain enters once again, to a ceremonial, circular 1881 phrase for horns, and proclaims that the lights of the city are to be extinguished in honour of the dead (all of this to music that seems to recall the Trial Scene in *Aida*). At the moment that Simone enters, the strings begin to slide upward in parallel chromatics [36], and we rejoin the 1857 version. It is an extraordinary sound in the early score: the whole scene is a kind of radicalizing of the Doge's

Howell Glynne as Fiesco and Arnold Matters as Boccanegra in the 1948 British première at Sadler's Wells, produced by John Moody, with sets by John Piper and costumes by Reginald Woolley (photo: Start Walter)

poisoning and dream-scene in Act Two. In the later score the chromatics take on even more significance as inversions of the Poison Motif [26]. The feverish Doge is momentarily refreshed by the sea-breeze [37] — again, airy string tremolos, a cool, trilling flute, and wave-rocked triple-time melodies, all so important to the musical atmosphere of the opera.

Fiesco suddenly emerges ('Era meglio per te!') to challenge his foe with fierce resolution, underscored by his initial insistence on a single pitch supported by rock-solid, but oscillating, 'modal' harmonies. (The Council Chamber Scene notwithstanding, Simone is not supposed to have seen — or at least recognized — Fiesco since the Prologue.) In several respects recalling the structure of the radical Simone-Fiesco duet in the Prologue, this second baritone-bass confrontation, largely from 1857, again expands the *tempo d'attacco* into a series of sectionalized contrasts. (As before, the dramatic point is to postpone the *adagio* in favour of prolonged dramatic

25

action: Verdi's resolute experimentalism in the later 1850s can scarcely be better exemplified than in these two duets.) Fiesco never sounds graver than at the beginning of the *tempo d'attacco* [38], an 'old-world' proclamation of Boccanegra's doom. Even the musical shape of Fiesco's eight lines, evoking the standard lyric-form pattern aa¹bc — but with all four phrases obsessively retaining the same dotted-rhythm figure until the final triplet-spilling concluding cadence — adds to the severity. After this initial proclamatory stanza the music breaks up into dialogue over thumping death-rhythms in the orchestra, as the lights of the piazza outside begin to be extinguished and Simone gradually recognizes Fiesco. In the forward-rushing 'Come un fantasima', still another section of the prolonged *tempo d'attacco*, Simone finally reveals to Fiesco (in a momentary shift to broadly arched 1881 music) that Amelia is his granddaughter. This leads to a tearful reconciliation, the duet's *adagio*. Fiesco's initially 'rhetorical' exposition [39] (compare the similarly E-flat minor openings of [22] and [32]) gives way not to a *risposta* in standard shape but to similarly rhetorical groundswells: the whole procedure seems to be more that of an ensemble reduced to two voices than that of a traditional duet. Towards the end of the *adagio* (the textual repetition of 'Vien, ch'io stringa al petto') we hear a new, rocking 'reconciliation theme', as the two link their voices together (Verdi had used this theme near the close of the 1857 Prelude). In the concluding section (the structure of the text suggests that it is a *tempo di mezzo* fused onto the end of the *adagio* as a kind of kinetic coda-pendant) Fiesco tells Simone that he is poisoned. As the 'reconciliation theme' swells up again in voice and orchestra, Simone requests to bless Amelia/Maria, whom he hears approaching with Gabriele and a respectful crowd of Genoese.

The final quartet, which the generally displeased Basevi judged in 1859 to be 'the most beautiful piece of the opera', begins with an initial section largely in recitative that passes quickly from happiness (Amelia's learning that Fiesco is her grandfather, and that Fiesco and Simone, through their joint relationship to her, have been reconciled) to sorrow (Simone reveals his imminent death). The more formal portion of the ensemble begins with Simone's nearly motionless blessing of his daughter and Gabriele [40] (notice the resemblance to the Preludes to Acts One and Three of *La traviata* as he mentions his 'martyrdom'). Rhythmic momentum is regained as Amelia and Gabriele respond sympathetically with parallel, similarly arched melodies. Fiesco, true to character, declares in a funereal four-measure shift to 1881 music that all earthly happiness is a deception. Finally, the Doge, gasping for breath, leads them all into a repeated, swelling *concertato* — much of it generously enriched in 1881. Instead of resolving at the end, the quartet-with-chorus crashes up against a *forte* diminished-seventh chord — a traditional musical symbol of disaster. The opera concludes with eight sombre lines from 1857 (the aim, similar, for instance, to that in the final five lines of *Il trovatore*, was to close the opera with a brief dramatic action: a '*tempo di mezzo*', but here with freer, *scena*-like poetry). Just before his death Simone chooses Gabriele to succeed him as Doge. Fiesco proclaims this to the people in the piazza outside. The last sounds — unusually quiet for Verdi, especially in 1857 — include ritual bell-strokes (compare the bells at the end of the Prologue) and the kneeling chorus gently praying for the dead Boccanegra in the dotted rhythms of a funeral march.

26

Verdi and his Singers
The vocal character of the two versions of 'Simon Boccanegra' in relation to the original casts

Desmond Shawe-Taylor

Among the innumerable comments on singers made by Verdi in the course of his long life, biographers and critics usually seize on those in which he speaks disparagingly of the species: expressing, for instance, his annoyance at the careless use of the word 'creator' to describe the first performer of a role. 'No', he said in a well-known letter to Giulio Ricordi (April 11, 1871); 'I want only one creator, and am satisfied if what is written is simply and correctly executed; the trouble is that this is never done. I often read in newspapers about "effects unimagined by the composer", but for my part I have never come across any of these.'

Conversely, biographers incline to overlook the equally numerous occasions when Verdi showed how much a particular singer had impressed or moved him. When the name of Gemma Bellincioni came up in 1886 as a possible Desdemona, the composer supported Boito's adverse view (January 23, 1886) against the enthusiasm of Ricordi; but a decade later we find him praising Bellincioni's famous Violetta, and sending her his photograph with the message 'To you who could give new life to the old sinner'. Thirty years before, there had been a pleasant and revealing little episode in his dealings with the famous baritone, Antonio Cotogni. Cotogni was suggested for the role of Rodrigo in the first Italian production of *Don Carlos* at Bologna in 1867; and Mariani, the conductor, brought him along to sing to Verdi. As a matter of fact, Verdi had already heard Cotogni four years earlier in a Madrid performance of *La forza del destino* which he described at the time as very poor except for the soprano and the tenor; but he may have forgotten this, and, if so, Cotogni, now 36 years old and approaching the peak of his career, might well have been too tactful to remind him.

Verdi accompanied the baritone at the piano in what Mariani calls Rodrigo's *aria di sortita* ('Carlo ch'è sol il nostro amore'), and then himself sang with Cotogni the Friendship Duet — 'with tenderness and exquisite finesse', says Mariani of the composer's vocal style. 'At the end of the piece', Mariani continues, 'the composer's face was lined with tears; the singer could count on a successful outcome.' You might say, perhaps, that Verdi was weeping at the beauty of his own singing — or, more probably, of his own music; but the implication of Mariani's words is that he was moved by Cotogni's voice and art. Cotogni himself had no doubt about the matter, if we may believe a slightly different account of the episode which the notoriously unreliable Gino Monaldi ascribed to the singer in his *Famous Singers of the Nineteenth Century*. The baritone is reported as having said that it was his singing of Rodrigo's death scene, 'io morrò, ma lieto in core', that had so affected Verdi, and moreover as attributing to the emotionally moved composer the uncharacteristic comment: 'You sing it, not as I wrote it — but no matter; by all means sing it like that since it goes splendidly so ... indeed, even better.'

We know also of Verdi's admiration for the Spanish tenor, Julián Gayarre,

27

whom he probably heard in 1876, and for the Italian heroic tenor, Gaetano Fraschini, whom he chose for four of his own operas between 1845 and 1859 (*Alzira*, *Il Corsaro*, *La Battaglia di Legnano* and *Un ballo in maschera*) and had in mind for one or two more; but the extravagant enthusiasm he is supposed to have expressed, as late as 1898, to the young Italian tenor, Alessandro Bonci, derives from a letter which is an evident forgery.[1]

The outstanding instance of his susceptibility to the singer's art is to be seen in his attitude to Patti — just the type of *prima donna assoluta* whose international renown and high-handed ways (she had a clause in her later contracts absolving her from attendance at all rehearsals of familiar operas) might have been expected to arouse in him some degree of hostility. In a letter (October 6, 1877) to Ricordi, however, he praises her extravagantly, describing her as 'a *born* artist in the full meaning of the word', and berating the complacent Milanese, Ricordi included, for having failed to appreciate her worth ten years before. From her performance in *Rigoletto* he singles out for his rapturous approval not her brilliant florid singing nor her pure cantabile, but the 'sublime effect' of her utterance of a single (usually unnoticed) phrase of recitative in the last act: Gilda's simple reply to her father's question near the beginning of the act: 'And you still love him?', 'I love him', 'Io l'amo'. On December 27, 1877, in a letter to Arrivabene, Verdi compares Patti very favourably with Malibran and goes on to describe her in still more rapturous terms: 'marvellous voice, very pure vocal style; a wonderful actress with a charm and naturalness such as no one else has!'

Historically, Verdi comes midway between an eighteenth-century composer like Mozart, who thought it natural to write roles and arias that should display to their best advantage whichever singers had been engaged, and the typical modern composer who, as a general rule, writes without any particular singer in mind. He was fond of enunciating as a maxim 'either operas for singers, or singers for operas' ('o le opere per cantanti, o i cantanti per l'opere')[2]. He seldom wrote parts specifically for this or that singer; but he always took careful note of the singers available, and avoided subjects that would give them roles beyond their powers. Thus, one of several reasons for his continually postponing the composition of *King Lear* was that there was often no baritone or bass in the proposed company who could safely be entrusted with so crucial and demanding a role as Lear, or else no soprano worthy of Cordelia.[3]

In the earlier part of his career, there are several instances of his writing fresh arias to suit a change of cast; and among the modifications that he made to *La traviata* for its second Venetian production, a year after the première at La Fenice, some were affected by the new singers — especially by the baritone, Filippo Coletti, who did not possess the exceptionally high range of Felice Varesi, the original Germont. Like all composers, in fact, Verdi usually had to be content with what was to hand; and then, as now, standards were very variable.

*

Of the two original casts for *Simon Boccanegra*, that of the Venice première of 1857 means less to us today than that of the Milan revision of 1881, for various reasons; partly because of the greater lapse of time, partly because the 1857 singers were perhaps not quite so famous as their Milanese successors of 1881, partly because two members of the later cast went on to achieve what may fairly be called immortality by becoming, six years later, the first Otello and

Carlo Negrini (left) the first Gabriele and Leone Giraldoni (right) the first Boccanegra, Venice 1857 (photos: Museo Teatrale alla Scala)

Iago, and partly because, later still, three of the four principals made primitive gramophone records.

Let us first glance, however, at the Venetian principals of 1857, several of whom were to repeat their roles elsewhere in Italy and abroad. The Boccanegra was Leone Giraldoni (1824–1897), a Frenchman in spite of his name, and father of the Eugenio Giraldoni who was to be Puccini's first Scarpia in 1900. Giraldoni *père* was by common consent a fine and unusually cultivated singer; Verdi admired him enough to entrust him, two years later, with the role of Renato in the first performance of *Un ballo in maschera* — although on that occasion, as at the time of *Simon Boccanegra*, his chronic tendency to ill-health was to prove troublesome. When about to repeat his Boccanegra in Rome in December 1857, Giraldoni wrote to Verdi asking for further guidance, to which Verdi rather testily (though not unreasonably) replied that, even if he had time, it would be pointless for him to write a long letter of instruction to a man who had sung the opera twice under his own direction, and very well too. He merely begged the baritone to avoid those *rallentandi* beloved by most singers but damaging to the music, adding for good measure that he desired all his singers, of either sex, to sing, and not to shout or declaim or scream. 'If in my music there are not many florid passages, there is no need on that account to tear your hair and rage like madmen.' As for Giraldoni himself, let him watch his health, and all will go well.

Verdi had reason to add this last injunction, for at the première both Giraldoni and Carlo Negrini (1826–1865), the tenor, had been ill and sang very badly, so we are told. Nothing much beyond vague general approval is heard of the bass, Giuseppe Echeverria (a Spaniard, one would suppose); but the soprano, Luigia Bendazzi (1833-1901), prompted a good deal of comment of one sort and another. Although she repeated her Amelia several times in various theatres and countries, we get the impression that she wasn't really suited to the character; she was what used to be called a *donna di forza*, and a famous Lady Macbeth, so that Verdi seems to have disregarded his own axiom in giving her the role of a modest girl. She was renowned for the power and fine quality of her voice, rather than for delicacy or purity of style. There survives an interesting letter written by the soprano, Marietta (or Maria) Piccolomini — a very celebrated Violetta of her day — to Giraldoni, undated but clearly written some time before the première, envying him and Negrini their good fortune in Verdi's having, as she puts it, 'written for them'; she herself longs to be the first to sing some Verdi opera (an ambition she was never to achieve, although Verdi wanted her particularly for the Cordelia of his unwritten *King Lear* and actually postponed its composition yet again, this time for Naples in 1856, because he couldn't get her).[4] Piccolomini assumes that the composer, having Bendazzi for his prima donna, had written for her a part 'tutta di forza', which wouldn't have suited her own talents at all.

The sound and thorough critic, Filippo Filippi, who in the course of his career reviewed the *Boccanegra* premières of both 1857 and 1881, thought that Bendazzi and Negrini were alike too violent and too declamatory for their music, adding that 'Verdi had not sacrificed or falsified the subject of his work by adapting it to the capacities of its first interpreters'. By the time Bendazzi sang Amelia at La Scala in 1859, her faults seem to have grown to the point at which they began to exasperate the audience, according to a long notice in the *Gazzetta Musicale di Milano* (unsigned, but possibly by Lambertini). Even in Venice two years before, says the writer, he had felt that she would ruin the great natural beauty of her voice by 'the exorbitance of her screams and the power of her attacks'. Evidently, something of the kind had by now happened, so that on the first night at La Scala she had quite a hostile reception; in consequence, she became so alarmed that on the second and third nights she went to the other extreme, not daring to sing out even where required, and sometimes merely 'buzzing like a fly'.

Curiously enough, the Amelia of the revised *Boccanegra*, Anna d'Angeri (1853-1907), a soprano of Austrian origin, aroused similar anxieties on the part of Verdi and Ricordi. The latter said that she would be vocally ideal: it was all a question of how far Verdi would get with her in matters of interpretation and personality — where, he remarked, 'you can sometimes work miracles'. Verdi thought that D'Angeri, precisely because of the power of her voice — and, he added, 'of her person' — would not be right for the part of a modest girl, quiet and frail, a kind of young nun; he doubted whether D'Angeri herself would feel quite happy with the part. For a while, Patti was considered, but Ricordi thought that here there were a good many 'cons' to balance the obvious 'pros': among them, Nicolini (Patti's second husband, a tenor), the enormous fees she would demand, and the fact that by now she was transposing all her pieces down, and could risk high notes only in florid passages, not in dramatic or accented phrases (this, be it observed, when the great soprano was no more than 37!). D'Angeri, at all events, was chosen, and she seems to have done pretty well; she was highly praised by Filippi, among others. Of course, the extensive changes in the role of Amelia — for instance, the omission of the Act One cabaletta — were the consequence of the

Luigia Bendazzi, who created the role of Amelia in Venice, 1857 (photo: Museo Teatrale alla Scala)

Victor Maurel (left) who sang Boccanegra and Francesco Tamagno (right) who sang Gabriele at La Scala, 1881 (photos: Museo Teatrale alla Scala)

composer's artistic development rather than of any difference in the new soprano's vocal powers as compared with those of her predecessor.

Only two months before the *Boccanegra* revival, and under the same conductor, Franco Faccio, there had been a highly successful *Ernani* at La Scala, with the identical four principals: D'Angeri (who according to Faccio, 'had a real ovation after her cavatina'), Francesco Tamagno (1850-1905), Victor Maurel (1848-1923) and Édouard de Reszke (1855-1917). Faccio praises them all. Maurel alone, he says, was not at his best on the first night because of a vocal indisposition, but on the second night he was splendid. Tamagno was 'excellent, with his exceptional voice and very powerful effects', while the sole complaint that could possibly be made of De Reszke would be that he sang *too* beautifully! These outstandingly successful *Ernani* performances served as a kind of run-in for the revised *Boccanegra*.

Tamagno's voice is still a living sound to many modern music-lovers from the thrilling records that he made of excerpts from *Otello*, *Guglielmo Tell* and other operas. Besides the power and beauty of his tone, he excelled in the clarity of his articulation: Tullio Serafin used to recall how Tito Ricordi would complain that on Tamagno nights the firm did badly in the sale of librettos, since no one bothered to buy one.[5] Tamagno was apparently the only one of the 1881 principals about whom there had been no casting doubts at any time. There was a moment when Verdi contemplated transposing Gabriele's aria up by a semitone because of Tamagno's brilliant upper register; but the composer was delighted when, after all, the change proved unnecessary. Joseph Kerman has plausibly suggested that in the Terzetto of Act Two the climactic high B flats on the words 'Dammi la morte', which were not in the first version, were inserted with Tamagno in mind. We may add that Gabriele's very striking phrase in the new finale to Act One, 'Pel cielo! uom possente sei tu!' (*lit.* 'By heavens! *You* are a man of power!), with its sudden leap to a high B flat sustained for more than a bar's length, is likewise ideally suited to Tamagno's trumpet tones. It has also been observed that in every act of the revised *Boccanegra* Gabriele's part rises to a higher note than in the first version: in Acts One and Three a semitone higher, in Act Two a whole tone higher. Here then, it may be, we have one of the relatively rare instances of Verdi's adapting one of his mature scores to suit a particular artist.

Strange as it may now seem, he was for some time dubious about the participation of both Maurel and De Reszke. For the role of Fiesco, he said, he wanted 'a voice of iron . . . a deep voice, effective down to the low F, with something in it of the inexorable, the prophetic, the sepulchral: all qualities not to be found in the somewhat hollow and baritonal voice of De Reszke.' His doubts about De Reszke's suitability to a role of this kind would have been shared by Bernard Shaw, who took the view (borne out by photographs) that the singer's stage personality was more jovial than formidable, and teased this supposedly spine-chilling Mephistopheles for 'his faith in the diabolic mockery of a smile that would make the most timid child climb straight up on his knee and demand to be shown how a watch opens when blown on.' Shaw considered that, as Marcel in *Les Huguenots*, De Reszke was a mere makeshift in the absence of a true *basso profondo*.[6] Nevertheless, De Reszke's repertory was that of a genuine bass. Besides Marcel, it included Gounod's Mephistopheles and Friar Lawrence, Mozart's Leporello, Beethoven's Rocco, Rossini's Don Basilio, Verdi's Ramfis, and Wagner's Daland, Hagen, King Henry and King Mark; only Hans Sachs (not one of his most admired parts) took him outside the regular bass regions. In *Les Huguenots* Marcel has three low Fs in the course of his big Act Three duet with Valentine (which Shaw found the best part of De Reszke's performance), and two of these can be heard — though too faintly to be of much value as evidence — in the fragments recorded on one of the 'Mapleson cylinders' from a live performance at the Metropolitan Opera House in 1903, with Johanna Gadski and Édouard De Reszke in the cast. Whether justified or not, Verdi's worries about De Reszke's range were eventually allayed, and the bass scored a great success. Filippi tells us that he sang 'Il lacerato spirito' divinely, and was so much applauded that (as can still too often happen) the lovely orchestral postlude to the aria was obscured; he had to give an encore of the piece.

Needless to say, by far the most important role is that of Simon Boccanegra himself. For him, said Verdi, we need 'a passionate spirit, most ardent, proud, with a calm and dignified exterior (something difficult to achieve) . . . We shan't find him, I know it well; but at least something approaching that.' At first he thought Maurel too young for the part. 'Voice, talent, sentiment — as much as you could ask, but never the calm composure and as it were theatrical authority indispensable for the part of Simone.' It is a role, the composer said, as tiring as Rigoletto, but a thousand times more difficult. In short, he wanted a paragon of all the virtues, both vocal and dramatic — and perhaps he found one after all. Maurel, says Filippi, was 'perfect, I dare to say sublime, both vocally and dramatically . . . the voice free and vigorous'; and he scored a very great success. Yet most commentators have agreed that his virtues were not predominantly vocal: he was no Battistini (a successful later Boccanegra at La Scala), no Cotogni, no Pandolfini. By the time he made his gramophone records (1903-1907), the voice itself was in sad decline, but much of his interpretative skill and charm can still be felt, especially in his singing of Iago's 'Era la notte' and in his famous 'Quand' ero paggio' from *Falstaff*.

At one point, Faccio tells us, Maurel had expressed fears regarding the high tessitura of *Simon Boccanegra*; but these problematical passages, the conductor tells Verdi, 'are precisely those which you have modified', so that Maurel is now reassured. The implication of Faccio's words is that Verdi had 'adjusted the part' to suit Maurel; but the changes, when examined, look more like simple compositional improvements which happened to lie more easily for the baritone's voice. Maurel was unusually intelligent; he passed for an intellectual among singers, who are not always a highly intellectual race. He painted a little, he was an architect, and a keen swordsman, and (dreadful thought) is said to have counted surgery among his hobbies; later on, he took up another lethal hobby, that of lecturing. According to the slightly equivocal phrase of Bernard Shaw, who speaks with authority on such a point, 'the role of lecturer was never better acted since lecturing began'.[7] During the eighties and nineties he published some half-dozen books or pamphlets, one of which was translated into German by the formidable Lilli Lehmann, while another was declared by Shaw to have been written in a style as clear as Tyndall's.[8] As Boccanegra, at all events, he surprised the doubting Verdi by his excellence[9], and must have particularly delighted him by making a huge success of the new finale to the first act.

Filippi's review repeats the story that already at one of the rehearsals the composer had exclaimed 'This is my Iago' — to which the critic appends the

Design for the 1881 production at La Scala, by Girolamo Magnani, showing the illuminated port through the arches of the Doge's palace (Museo Teatrale alla Scala)

34

comment: 'If Verdi said so, he had excellent reason.' And the story seems to be true that at another rehearsal the composer so far forgot himself as to say to his baritone something that was rather out of keeping with his usual cautious attitude towards singers, namely: 'If God gives me strength, I'll write *Iago* for you!' When we recall that Tamagno was to be his first Otello, and Maurel also his first Falstaff, we can see at La Scala a performing tradition of unusual consistency stretching from the *Ernani* revival of early 1881, through the *Simon Boccanegra* revision and the revised *Don Carlos* of 1884 with Tamagno in the title role, followed by the Pantaleoni/Tamagno/Maurel/Navarrini *Aida* of late 1886[10] to the twin final summits of Verdi's long and glorious career, the *Otello* of 1887 and the *Falstaff* of 1893.

Notes

1   A supposed letter of Verdi to Bonci of May 21, 1898, quoted in G. Lauri-Volpi, *Voci parallele*, (Milan, 1955), 132, and elsewhere, expresses 'al bravo tenore Bonci' (then aged 28) the 84-year-old composer's 'most welcome surprise' ('graditissima sorpresa'), after hearing the tenor's famous touches of inserted laughter in the quintet 'È scherzo od è follia' (*Un ballo in maschera*). The wholly spurious nature of this letter has been clearly shown by Arnaldo Marchetti in 'La famosa lettera di Verdi a Bonci', *Rassegna Musicale Curci*, n. 3/xii.1973.23-4. I owe this reference to the kindness of Dr Giorgio Gualerzi; and to Andrew Porter a further, and seemingly decisive, reference to a letter of Verdi to Escudier of March 11, 1865, in which the composer dismisses the notion that an operatic Lady Macbeth might employ (as the actress Ristori did) a death-rattle in the throat, adding: 'In music, that must and cannot be done; just as one shouldn't cough in the last act of *La traviata*; or laugh in the "scherzo od è follia" of *Ballo in Maschera*' (quoted in *Verdi's Macbeth: A Sourcebook*, edited by David Rosen and Andrew Porter (Cambridge, 1984), 110).

2   F. Abbiati, Giuseppe Verdi: (Milan, 1959), iv. 132. *Cf* Gatti, Verdi (Milan, 1951), ii. 79: 'ed opere adatte agli artisti ed artisti addati alle opere', where Verdi seems to demand, underlining his phrase, not one or the other of these two conditions, but both at once.

3   The chequered story of Verdi's many returns to the *King Lear* project, and of his reasons or excuses for its postponement and eventual abandonment, is conveniently summarised in V. Godefroy, *The Dramatic Genius of Verdi*, ii. (London, 1977), 327-348, and in C. Osborne, *The Complete Operas of Verdi*, (London, 1969), 77-82.

4   Verdi to V. Torelli, November 11, 1856, in *Copialettere*, 196-7. He was also prepared to accept, for Cordelia, Virginia Boccabadati or Maria Spezia: 'all three have weak voices but great talent, soul (*anima*) and stage-sense. All are excellent in *La traviata*'. For the Fool he insists on the contralto, Giuseppina Brambilla. In a further letter to Torelli (December 7, 1856, in *Copialettere*, 197) he absolutely declines Penco for Cordelia, adding that he would not have singers *foisted* upon him, 'not even if Malibran were to return from the grave'.

5   T. Serafin, 'Tre Cantanti' in *Discoteca*, anno II, no. 10, 15, vii.1961. Emma Eames, who often sang the role of Desdemona to Tamagno's Otello, once replied to a question of my own about the quality of his voice, 'Short of having a silver trumpet in his throat, he could not have sung more wonderfully'.

6   B. Shaw, *Music in London 1890-94*, Standard Edition, (London, 1932), i. 172, 199.

7   Shaw, *op. cit.*, i.99

8   Shaw, *op. cit.*, ii. 138

9   Verdi to G. Piroli, 5.iv.1881, in Abbiati, *op. cit.*, iv, 155: 'Maurel is a Simon Boccanegra whose equal I shall never see'.

10 Romilda Pantaleoni and Francesco Navarrini were the first interpreters of Desdemona and Lodovico in *Otello*.

Thematic Guide

Many of the themes from this opera have been identified in the articles by numbers in square brackets, which refer to the themes set out on these pages. The themes are also identified by the numbers in square brackets at the corresponding points in the libretto, so that the words can be related to the musical themes.

[1]
Allegro moderato

[2] Moderato

[3]
Allegro moderato
PAOLO *sotto voce*

See the Pa - laz - zo Fie - schi?
L'a - tra ma - gion ve - de - te?

[4]
CHORUS (tenors) *dolcissimo*

And ev'- ry soul who pas - ses has tried in vain to see her,
Pas - san - do ogni pie - to - so in - van mi-rar de - si - a,

[5]
Andante sostenuto
FIESCO

God broke a ten - der fath - er's heart.
Il la - ce - ra - to spi - ri - to

[6] Allegro agitato
FIESCO *con forza*

Fate must be blind to have brought you her be - fore me
Qual cie - co fa - to a oltraggiar - mi ti tra - e - a?

[7] Andantino
SIMONE *cantabile*

On a far sea - shore
Del mar sul li - do

[8] AMELIA *cantabile*

Oh, __ how the stars are shi __ ning,
Co __ me in que-st'o - ra bru - na

[9] Più mosso
GABRIELE

(A) sky __ when no stars are shi __ ning,
Cie - lo di stel-le or - ba - to,

[10] Andantino
AMELIA *cantabile*

p Turn back your mind to de - light then,
Ri - pa - ra i tuo - i pen - sie - - ri,

[11] Allegro brillante
AMELIA *molto piano per quattro battute*

Now let's re-joice in hap - pi - ness
Sì, sì, del-l'a-ra il giu - bi - lo

[12]
Sostenuto religioso
FIESCO

[13]
GABRIELE *con espressione*

Come, my son, and kneel before me __
Vie - ni a me, ti be-ne-di - co

Now I feel the voice of an an-cient time
E-co pi - a del tem-po an ti - co

[14] *from Amelia/Simone duet, Act One*
Allegro giusto

[15] Andantino
AMELIA

pp

I was raised as a hum - ble or - phan
Or-fa - nel-la il tet - to u - mi - le

37

[16] Andantino
AMELIA

Oh how bit - ter, oh how bit - ter,
Co - me tri - ste, co - me tri - ste,

[17] Allegro giusto
SIMONE

[18] AMELIA *più mosso con espress.*

Daughter! My heart leaps at the word!
Fi - glia! a tal no - me pal - pi - to!

Fa-ther, you'll see me al - ways there
Pa - dre, ve-drai la vi - gi - le

[19] *Finale Primo 1*
Allegro moderato

[20a] Allegro agitato

pp sotto voce

[20b] CHORUS

Ran - sack and pil - lage!
Ar - mi! sac - cheg - gio!

[21] Cantabile
AMELIA *dolcissimo*

The eve-ning was fal - ling, the air was en-chan - ting
Nel - l'o - ra so - a - ve'che all'e - sta-si in - vi - ta

[22] Andante mosso
SIMONE *con maesta*

Peo-ple! Pa-tri-cians! Pro-ge-ny of a fe-ro-cious his-tory
Ple-be! Pa-tri-zii! Po - po-lo dal-la fe-ro - ce sto-ria!

[23] Meno mosso
SIMONE

All that I ask ·is peace, now! All that I ask is love!
e vo gri-dan-do: pa - ce! e vo gri-dan-do:a-mor!

[24]
AMELIA *dolcissimo*

animando   a tempo

Calm _____ now! Oh let me beg you give up your fierce dis-dain!
Pa - ce! lo sdegno immen - so nas-con-di per pie - tà!

[25] Largo assai

ff   *tutta forza*

[26] SIMONE *(terribly)*

(darkly and terribly to Paolo)

He's cursed for e — ver! Now you _ re-peat the oath.
Sia ma-le-det - to! e tu _ ri-peti il giu-ro.

a poco a poco string.

(etc.)

ff ————— *ppp*

(poison /revenge)

[27] Allegro sostenuto
FIESCO

Tell me, where are you lead-ing me pris'-ner?
Pri-gio-niero in qual lo-co m'ad - du-ci?

[28] Allegro sostenuto
GABRIELE *con forza*

3

Ah, see how a burn-ing jea - lous-y
Sen-to av-vam-par nel - l'a - ni-ma

[29] Largo
GABRIELE *con espress.*

Come now, my love, come back to me,
Cie - lo pieto - so, ren-di-la,

[30] Andante
GABRIELE *con espressione*

Give me a rea - son why I should
Par-la,in tuo cor vir-gi - ne-o

[31] Allegro agitato
AMELIA

pp 3   3   3

You would kill __ an old man _ when he's sleep - ing?
Vecchio iner - me il tuo brac - cio col - pi - sce?

[32] Andante sostenuto
GABRIELE *con espress.*

For-give, for-give, A - me-lia,
Per - don, per-don, A - me-lia,

39

[33] GABRIELE *accentate*

Put me to death then, put me to death ___ then;
Dammi la mor - te, dammi la mor — te;

[34] Allegro assai
CHORUS
pp

To bat - tle now, Li - gu - ri - a, your sa - cred du - ty calls you.
Al - l'ar - mi, all'ar - mi, o Li - gu - ri, sa - cro do - ver v'ap - pel - la.

[35]
PAOLO

It was my de - mon sent me in - to bat - tle
Il mio de - mo - nio mi cacciò fra l'ar - mi

[36] Moderato
SIMONE

Fire in my tem - ples _
M'ar - don le tem - pia _

[37] Moderato
SIMONE

The salt ___ wind! The salt ___ wind!
Il ma - re! Il ma - re!

[38] Largo
FIESCO

By the fes - ti - val tor - ches that glit - ter
Del - le fa - ci fes - tan - ti al bar - lu - me

[39] Largo
FIESCO *con espressione*
p

I weep be - cause there speaks to me
Pian - go, per - chè mi par - la

[40] Andante sostenuto assai
SIMONE
pp

Al - might - y Lord of Hea - ven, Look down on them and bless them;
Gran Dio, li be - ne - di - ci pie - to - so dall'em - pi - ro;

40

Simon Boccanegra

An Opera in a Prologue and Three Acts
by Giuseppe Verdi

Libretto by Francesco Maria Piave, with additions by Giuseppe
Montanelli, after the play *Simón Boccanegra* by Antonio García
Gutiérrez, and with additions and alterations for the revised
version by Arrigo Boito

English translation of the 1881 libretto by James Fenton

Simon Boccanegra was first performed in four acts at the Teatro La
Fenice, Venice, on March 12, 1857. The opera was then revised and
the first performance of this second version, divided into a prologue
with three acts, was at the Teatro alla Scala, Milan, on March 24,
1881. The first performance in the United States of the revised
version was at the Metropolitan Opera House, New York, on January
28, 1932. The first performance in England was at Sadler's Wells
Theatre on October 28, 1948.

The main text given here, and translated for performance by James
Fenton, is the 1881 revised version of the libretto. In the footnotes and
at the end of the text the different lines and scenes in the 1857 libretto
are set out with references to Julian Budden's chapter on the opera in
The Operas of Verdi (Vol. 2) and literal translations by Sylvia
Mulcahy.

The stage directions are literal translations of the original directions
in the librettos, and do not represent any particular production. The
numbers in square brackets refer to the Thematic Guide.

CHARACTERS

Prologue

Simon Boccanegra *corsair in the service of the Genoese republic*	*baritone*
Jacopo Fiesco *a Genoese noble*	*bass*
Paolo Albiani *a Genoese goldsmith*	*baritone*
Pietro *a popular leader*	*baritone*

Opera

Simon Boccanegra *Doge of Genoa*	*baritone*
Maria Boccanegra *his daughter, under the name of Amelia*	*soprano*
Jacopo Fiesco *under the name of Andrea*	*bass*
Gabriele Adorno *a Genoese gentleman*	*tenor*
Paolo *a courtier, the Doge's favourite*	*baritone*
Pietro *another courtier*	*baritone*
A maidservant of Amelia	*mezzo-soprano*

Soldiers, Sailors, Artisans, Populace, Servants of Fiesco, Senators, the Doge's Court, African prisoners* of both sexes.

The action takes place in and around Genoa towards the middle of the fourteenth century. Between the Prologue and the Opera twenty-five years pass.

* Only in 1857, because in 1881 the ballet was cut.

Prologue

A square in Genoa. In the background the church of San Lorenzo. To the right the Palazzo dei Fieschi with a large balcony: set in the wall beside the balcony is an image of the Virgin in front of which burns a small lamp. To the left other houses. Several streets lead into the square. It is night. [1]

Scene One. *Paolo and Pietro are on stage, conversing. / The whole scene to be sung mezza voce.*

PAOLO

You'd elect him for the leader of the people?   Che dicesti? . . . all'onor di primo abate
Lorenzino the usurer?   Lorenzin, l'usuriere? . . .

PIETRO

Suggest another more worthy figure.   Altro proponi
     Di lui più degno!

PAOLO

A hero — one who fought the pirates   Il prode che dai nostri
And chased them from our seas for ever,   Mari cacciava l'african pirata,
And gave the name Liguria   E al ligure vessillo
All of the honour of her ancient standard.   Rese l'antica nominanza altera.

PIETRO

I'm with you . . . and the payment?   Intesi . . . e il premio?

PAOLO

Riches and power and honour.   Oro, possanza, onore.

PIETRO

Thus will I sell the favour of the people.   Vendo a tal prezzo il popolar favore.

They clasp hands. Pietro leaves.

Scene Two.

PIETRO
(raising his voice a little, but not too much)

O detested patricians,   Abborriti patrizi,
You shall see me ascend the heights of power,   Alle cime ove alberga il vostro orgoglio,
Though by birth I'm a low despised plebeian.   Disprezzato plebeo, salire io voglio.

Scene Three. *Simon enters hurriedly.*

SIMONE
(expansively, then mezza voce)

I embrace you . . . What's happened?   Un amplesso . . . Che avvenne? — Da Savona
You have called me from Savona to see you.   Perchè qui m'appellasti?

PAOLO
(mysteriously)

Tomorrow do you wish to be made our leader?   All'alba eletto
     Esser vuoi nuovo abate?

SIMONE

Me? No.   Io? No.

43

PAOLO

The crown of the Doge should tempt you.   Ti tenta

                    Ducal corona?

SIMONE

What madness!   Vaneggi?

PAOLO
(*meaningfully*)

        Or Maria?   E Maria?

SIMONE
(*passionately*)

The innocent who suffered   O vittima innocente
From the blight of my passion?   Del funesto amor mio!
                                         (*speaking*)
Tell me, what news of her?   Dimmi, di lei
Have you two spoken?   Che sai? Le favellasti?

PAOLO
(*pointing to the Palazzo dei Fieschi*)

        She's imprisoned there   Prigioniera
In that very house ...   Geme in quella magion ...

SIMONE

        Maria!   Maria!

PAOLO

But who could deny her to the Doge?   Negarla

                    Al Doge chi potria?

SIMONE

Pitiful!   Misera!

PAOLO

        You're tempted?   Assenti?

SIMONE

Paolo ...   Paolo ...

PAOLO

I've seen to everything ... and all I ask   Tutto disposi ... e sol ti chieggo
You is for a share of danger and power ...   Parte ai perigli e alla possanza ...

SIMONE

So be it ...   Sia ...

PAOLO

You swear by your life then?   In vita e in morte?

SIMONE

        So be it.   Sia ...

PAOLO

Conceal yourself ... they're coming ...   S'appressa alcun ... T'ascondi ...
Just for a while we must maintain the   Per poco ancor, mistero ne circondi.
  mystery.

        Simone goes off. Paolo stands aside near the Palazzo dei Fieschi. [2]

Scene Four. *Paolo, Pietro, sailors and artisans enter gradually.*

PIETRO
(*mezza voce*)

Tomorrow, early, we'll assemble.   All'alba tutti qui verrete?

44

SAILORS AND ARTISANS

Early!   Tutti!

PIETRO

None for the patricians?   Niun pei patrizi?

SAILORS AND ARTISANS

No one.   Niuno. — A Lorenzino
We're all decided we should choose   Tutti il voto darem.
Lorenzino.

PIETRO

He's bought by the Fieschi.   Venduto è ai Fieschi.

SAILORS AND ARTISANS

So who should we elect then?   Dunque chi fia l'eletto?

PIETRO

A hero.   Un prode.

SAILORS AND ARTISANS

Yes.   Sì.

PIETRO

And one of us.   Un popolan . . .

SAILORS AND ARTISANS

Well spoken . . . do you know   Ben dici . . . ma fra i nostri
Such a man?   Sai l'uom?

PIETRO

Yes.   Sì.

SAILORS AND ARTISANS

Then who? Proclaim his name!   E chi? . . . Risuoni il nome suo!

PAOLO
(coming forward)

Simone Boccanegra.   Simone Boccanegra.

SAILORS AND ARTISANS
(with a cry, then suddenly sotto voce)

Simone? The pirate?   Simone? il Corsaro?

PAOLO

Yes . . . yes . . . the pirate for our leader. Sì . . . il Corsaro all'alto scranno.

SAILORS AND ARTISANS

He's here?   È qui?

PAOLO

He'll come.   Verrà.

SAILORS AND ARTISANS

And the Fieschi?   E i Fieschi?

PAOLO

They'll keep silent.   Taceranno.
He gathers everybody around him, then, pointing to the Palazzo dei Fieschi, says mysteriously and sotto voce . . .
See the Palazzo Fieschi, black as the souls [3]   L'atra magion vedete? . . . de' Fieschi è
who wrought it —   l'empio ostello,
There weeps a beautiful woman, buried   Una beltà infelice geme sepolta in quello;
within its quarters.

45

If you should pause to listen, only her lamentations	Sono i lamenti suoi la sola voce umana
Sound from the mausoleum of her incarceration.	Che risuonar s'ascolta nell'ampia tomba arcana.

PIETRO, SAILORS AND ARTISANS
(sotto voce)

Three months have passed already since that most noble person	Già volgono tre lune, che la gentil sembianza,
Appeared to grace the window of her deserted prison.	Non rallegrò i veroni della romita stanza;
And every soul who passes has tried in vain [4] to see her:	Passando ogni pietoso invan mirar desia
The miserable beauty, the prisoner Maria.	La bella prigioniera, la misera Maria.

PAOLO

Only a proud patrician passes within those portals . . .	Si schiudon quelle porte solo al patrizio altero,
Given to arts of mystery known to such evil mortals.	Che ad arte si ravvolge nell'ombre del mistero . . .

SAILORS AND ARTISANS

It's true then.	È vero.

PAOLO

But when the night is darkest, there is a light that wanders	Ma vedi in notte cupa per le deserte sale
Through the deserted mansion: it seems a soul in torment.	Errar sinistra vampa, qual d'anima infernale.

SAILORS AND ARTISANS

Oh heaven! Oh heaven! Gran Dio!	Oh cielo! Oh cielo! Gran Dio!
A cavern for a haunted soul! . . . Horror and fear!	Par l'antro de' fantasimi! . . . Oh qual orror! . . .

The reflection of a light is seen in the palace.

PAOLO

Look up there!	Guardate!
The haunting light is moving . . .	La feral vampa appare . . .

SAILORS AND ARTISANS

Oh heaven!	Oh ciel!

PAOLO

Now keep your distance.	V'allontanate.
And cross yourselves thrice over to exorcise the demon.	Si caccino i demonii col segno della croce . . .

SAILORS AND ARTISANS

We cross ourselves thrice over to exorcise the demon.	Si caccino i demonii col segno dalla croce . . .

PAOLO

Tomorrow.	All'alba.

SAILORS AND ARTISANS

Here.	Qui.

PIETRO

Simone.	Simone.

SAILORS AND ARTISANS

Simon for our leader.	Simone ad una voce.

All leave in groups, in different directions.

Scene Five. *Fiesco comes out of the palace.*

FIESCO

I bid farewell for ever, my noble palace,	A te l'estremo addio, palagio altero,
Now you're the tomb of my angel Maria!	Freddo sepolcro dell'angiolo mio!
For I failed to protect her! Oh, how I curse	Nè a proteggerti valsi! . . . Oh maledetto! . . .
him — the cowardly seducer!	oh vile seduttore! . . .
And you, Virgin, allowed it.	E tu, Vergin, soffristi

(*turning towards the image of the Virgin*)

Was it your plan that my daughter lost her virtue?	Rapita a lei la verginal corona? . . .
Ah, to say that! . . . That's madness! . . .	Ah! che dissi? . . . deliro! . . . ah mi
Ah, grant me pardon!	perdona!
God broke a tender father's heart, [5]	Il lacerato spirito
Drove his poor soul to madness.	Del mesto genitore
God kept me for the torture	Era serbato a strazio
Of infamy and sadness.	D'infamia e di dolore.

And Heaven in Its mercy gave	Il serto a lei de' martiri
A martyr's crown to thee.	Pietoso il cielo diè . . .
Risen to where the angels shine,	Resa al fulgor degli angeli,
Pray now, Maria, for me.	Prega, Maria, per me.

Mourning is heard from inside the palace.

WOMEN

Maria! Maria! The heavens now receive her!	È morta! È morta! . . . a lei s'apron le sfere!
But we shall never meet on this earth, we shall not meet again.	Mai più! Mai più non la vedremo in terra!

MEN

Miserere! . . . Miserere! . . .	Miserere! . . . Miserere! . . .

People come out of the palace and, sadly crossing the square, go away.

Scene Six. *Simone returns exultantly to the stage.*

SIMONE

Now every voice calls out my name. O Maria,	Suona ogni labbro il mio nome. O Maria,
In a short while	Forse in breve potrai
You may call me your husband!	Dirmi tuo sposo!

(*seeing Fiesco*)

Someone's watching! Who is it?	Alcun veggo! . . . chi fia?

FIESCO

Simon?	Simon?

SIMONE

You!	Tu!

FIESCO

Fate must be blind [6]	Qual cieco fato
To have brought you here before me.	A oltraggiarmi ti traea? . . .
I was calling on your head	Sul tuo capo io qui chiedea
The fatal wrath of Heaven above.	L'ira vindice del ciel.

SIMONE

O my father, now forgive me . . .	Padre mio, pietà t'imploro
I'm a suppliant here before you.	Supplichevole a' tuoi piedi . . .
Oh forgive me, I implore you . . .	Il perdono a me concedi . . .

FIESCO

It's too late.	Tardi è omai.

47

SIMONE

Don't be so cruel.	Non sii crudel.
All I wanted was to rise	Sublimarmi a lei sperai
On the pinions of my glory,	Sovra l'ali della gloria,
That my trophies could be laid	Strappai serti alla vittoria
Upon the altar of my love!	Per l'altare dell'amor!

FIESCO
(coldly)

I admire your reckless courage,	Io fea plauso al tuo valore,
But the offence I cannot pardon ...	Ma le offese non perdono ...
If I see you come to power —	Te vedessi asceso al trono ...

SIMONE

Silence ...	Taci ...

FIESCO

— you will earn my hatred.	Segno all'odio mio
Heaven's curse will fall upon you,	E all'anátema di Dio
You who dared to take my child.	È di Fiesco l'offensor.

SIMONE

Peace now ...	Pace ...

FIESCO

No! Peace will not come now	No! — pace non fora
Till one of us destroys the other.	Se pria l'un di noi non mora.

SIMONE

Would my blood placate your anger?	Vuoi col sangue mio placarti?

(baring his breast)

Strike me here then ...	Qui ferisci ...

FIESCO
(drawing back proudly)

You beg for murder?	Assassinarti? ...

SIMONE

Yes, you can kill me, and when I'm buried	Si, m'uccidi, e almen sepolta
You can end this anger ...	Fia con me tant'ira ...

FIESCO

Now hear me.	Ascolta:
If you want to earn my pardon,	Se concedermi vorrai
You must give to me the daughter,	L'innocente sventurata
The offspring of your wicked love.	Che nascea d'impuro amor,
Though I've never seen my grandchild,	Io, che ancor non la mirai,
Still I swear I'll make her happy,	Giuro renderla beata,
And I swear I'd pardon you.	E tu avrai perdono allor.

SIMONE

No, I cannot!	Nol poss'io!

FIESCO

Why not?	Perchè?

SIMONE

A wretched fate	Rubella
Took her away ...	Sorte lei rapi ...

FIESCO

You're lying.	Favella.

On a far sea-shore, in a strange country, [7]	Del mar sul lido fra gente ostile;
She grew up hidden from hostile people;	Crescea nell'ombra quella gentile;
She was so helpless far from her father.	Crescea lontana dagli occhi miei,
There was an aged woman to guard her.	Vegliava annosa donna su lei.
One time I went there at nightfall,	Di là una notte varcando, solo
Left my ship on my own and went off to meet her.	Dalla mia nave scesi a quel suolo.
I ran to find her ... there was no answer.	Corsi alla casa ... n'era la porta
The house was empty.	Serrata, muta!

FIESCO

The woman?	La donna?

SIMONE

Dead!	Morta!

FIESCO

What of your daughter?	E la tua figlia?

SIMONE

Three days she wandered	Misera, trista,
Wretched and lonely, three days she cried	Tre giorni pianse, tre giorni errò;
And then she vanished. Nobody saw her.	Scomparve poscia, nè fu più vista,
Since then in vain I've searched for my child.	D'allora indarno cercata io l'ho.

FIESCO

If you can't meet my wishes in this	Se il mio desire compir non puoi,
There can be no more peace between us!	Pace non puote esser fra noi!
Farewell, forever ...	Addio, Simone ...

He turns his back on Simon.

SIMONE

I will placate you,	Coll'amor mio
You know I love you. Hear me, oh hear me.	Saprò placarti; m'odi, ah m'odi.

FIESCO
(coldly and without turning)

No.	No.

SIMONE

Hear me.	M'odi.

FIESCO

Farewell now.	Addio.

He walks away, and then steps aside to watch.

SIMONE

Oh, the vicious and proud race of the Fieschi!	Oh de' Fieschi implacata, orrida razza!
And was it from such animals	E tra cotesti rettili nascea
That beauty I love so was born? I want to see her ...	Quella pura beltà? ... Vederla voglio ...
I have to!	Coraggio!
(He goes to the palace gate and knocks three times.)	
Silence in the house of the Fieschi?	Muta è la magion de' Fieschi?
The doors are standing open!	Dischiuse son le porte! ...
What can have happened? I'll see.	Quale mistero! ... entriam.

He goes into the palace resolutely.

Go in — embrace the corpse
Of your loved one.

T'inoltra e stringi
Gelida salma.

SIMONE
(*appearing on the balcony*)

It's empty!   Nessuno!... qui sempre
Just shadows and silence everywhere ...   Silenzio e tenebra!
(*He unfastens the lamp from the shrine and re-enters. His cry is heard from within.*)
Maria!... Maria!   Maria!... Maria!

FIESCO

The time has come for retribution.   L'ora suono del tuo castigo ...

SIMONE
(*leaving the place in terror*)

I'm dreaming!   È sogno!...
Yes, I am dreaming! What fearful things   Si; spaventoso, atroce sogno il mio!
I'm seeing!

VOICES OF THE POPULACE
(*in the distance*)

Boccanegra!...   Boccanegra!...

SIMONE

Those voices!   Quai voci!

VOICES OF THE POPULACE
(*approaching*)

Boccanegra!   Boccanegra!

SIMONE

These are the sounds of Hell!   Eco d'inferno è questo!...

Scene Seven. *Enter hurriedly Paolo and Pietro with several sailors and artisans.*

PAOLO AND PIETRO

All the people have acclaimed you!   Doge il popol t'acclama!

SIMONE

Leave me, you spirits — leave me!   Via fantasmi! via!

PAOLO AND PIETRO

What do you say?   Che di' tu?...

SIMONE

Paolo! There... a coffin!   Paolo!... Ah!... una tomba ...

PAOLO

A throne!   Un trono!

FIESCO
(*aside*)

They've chosen Simon? Hell lights its   Doge Simon?... m'arde l'inferno in petto!
flames within me!

POPULACE
(*crowding in with lighted torches*)

Viva Simon — elected by the people!!!   Viva Simon, del popolo l'eletto!!!

The bells ring out in celebration.

End of the Prologue.

Act One

The garden of the Grimaldi palace outside Genoa. On the left the palace, in front the sea. Dawn is breaking.

Scene One. / *Cavatina.*

AMELIA
(looking towards the sea)

Oh, how the stars are smiling,	[8] Come in quest'ora bruna
The sea is dark and friendly!	Sorridon gli astri e il mare!
Oh, how the moon is shining,	Come s'unisce, o luna,
To touch the crest of the wave — Ah!	All'onda il tuo chiaror! Ah!
It seems to nestle gently —	Amante amplesso pare
Like tender hearts in love.	Di due verginei cor!
But how can starlight soften,	Ma gli astri e la marina
And how can water comfort,	Che dicono alla mente
The sorrows of an orphan	Dell'orfana meschina?
When nightfall darkens her soul?	La notte atra, crudel,
Think of the dying woman's last words:	Quando la pia morente
God keep you well!	Sclamò: ti guardi il ciel!
O noble ancient dwelling,	O altero ostel, soggiorno
The home of the proud Grimaldi,	Di stirpe ancor più altera,
I'll not forget the humble	Il tetto disadorno
Home where I used to be! — Ah!	Non obliai per te!... Ah!
Only in your pomp and grandeur	Solo in tua pompa austera
Will love be good to me.	Amor sorride a me.

She turns again to the sea. Day breaks.[1]

The sky is grey, I have not heard	S'inalba il ciel, ma l'amoroso canto
My lover come singing sweetly!...	Non s'ode ancora!...
Every day he will sing, just as the dawn	Ei mi terge ogni dì, come l'aurora
Dries off the dew from the flowers, he cures my sorrow.	La rugiada dei fior, del ciglio il pianto.

Scena and Duet.

GABRIELE
(in the distance)

A sky when no stars are shining,	[9] Cielo di stelle orbato,
A field where flowers are dying,	Di fior vedovo prato,
Is a soul devoid of love.	È l'alma senza amor.

---

[1] In the 1857 version of the opera, this scene ended with a recitative and cabaletta.

AMELIA

Day has broken!... He has not come!... Maybe some mishap ...	Spuntò il giorno!... Ei non vien!... Forse sventura ...
Perhaps another love!... No, it would be against the will of God!...	Forse altro amor!... No, nol consenta Iddio!...
My soul tells me so!... He loves me! He is my faithful love.	L'alma mel dice!... Ei m'ama! È il fido mio.

GABRIELE
(from afar)

[A sky when no stars are shining,	Cielo di stelle orbato,
A field where flowers are dying,	Di fior vedovo prato,
Is a soul devoid of love.]	È l'alma senza amor.

AMELIA

[Heaven!... It's his voice!... It's him!...	Ciel!... la sua voce!... È desso!
He is approaching! ... How glorious!...]	Ei s'avvicina!... oh gioia!...
'The whole world smiles upon me now!...'	'Tutto m'arride l'universo adesso!...'

51

AMELIA

Heaven! . . . It's his voice! . . . It's him! . . .	Ciel! . . . la sua voce! . . . È desso! . . .
He is approaching! . . . How glorious! . . .	Ei s'avvicina! . . . oh gioia! . . .

GABRIELE
(approaching)

Without a heart to cherish,	Se manca un cor che t'ama,
All wealth and honour perish,	Non empiono tua brama
Power can never move.	Oro, possanza, onor.

AMELIA

He's here! . . . With love	Ei vien! . . . l'amor
My soul's aflame,	M'avvampa in sen
My tender heart	E spezza il fren
Will burst with joy!	L'ansante cor!

Scene Two. *Amelia and Gabriele entering from the right.*

GABRIELE

Oh, let me see you!	Anima mia!

AMELIA

But what could have delayed you?	Perchè si tardi giungi?

GABRIELE

Forgive me, dearest . . . These long delays on my part	Perdona, o cara . . . I lunghi indugi miei
Will help to bring you greatness . . .	T'apprestano grandezza . . .

AMELIA

I'm frightened . . .	Pavento . . .

GABRIELE

Why?	Chè?

AMELIA

I know of all your secrets . . .	L'arcano tuo conobbi . . .
You have prepared my grave,	A me sepolcro appresti,
And the gallows for you! . . .	Il patibolo a te! . . .

GABRIELE

What is this?	Che pensi?

Footnote ¹ continued.

GABRIELE

[Without a heart to cherish,	Se manca il cor che t'ama
All wealth and honour perish,]	Non empiono tua brama
Jewels, power, honour.	Gemme, possanza, onor.

AMELIA

This trembling must be stilled,	Il palpito deh frena,
O loving heart,	O core innamorato,
On this blessed day,	In questo dì beato,
No, I would not wish to die.	No, non vorrei morir.
Like a rainbow	Ad iride somiglia
Is his sweet voice to me,	La dolce sua parola,
Which alone in the world	Che in terra puote sela
Could calm my sighs.	Calmare i miei sospir.

Scene Two. *Gabriele enters from the right.*

AMELIA

At last I see you —	Ti veggo alfin —
[But what could have delayed you?] (*etc.*)	Perchè si tardi giungi?

52

AMELIA

I love
Andrea as a father, you know it,
Still I'm so frightened!... Have I not
Seen you here in the night? —
You meet together, in the darkest shadows,
Furtively and in silence.

Io amo
Andrea qual padre, il sai;
Pur m'atterrisce!... In cupa
Notte non vi mirai
Sotto le tetre volte errar sovente
Torbidi, irrequieti?

GABRIELE

Who?

Chi?

AMELIA

You and Andrea,
And Lorenzino and the others.

Tu, e Andrea,
E Lorenzino ed altri.

GABRIELE

Ah, silence ... the wind
Could be carrying our voices to the tyrant!
The walls have ears ... informers are concealed
In every cranny ...

Ah taci ... il vento
Ai tiranni potria recar tai voci!
Parlan le mura ... un delator s'asconde

Ad ogni passo ...

AMELIA

You tremble? ...

Tu tremi? ...

GABRIELE

If you'd only
Dispel these phantoms!

I funesti
Fantasmi scaccia!

AMELIA

You speak now of phantoms?

Fantasmi dicesti?

Come and admire: the sea is blue;
Look how the waves are dancing;
See how the towers of Genoa
Rise out of the foam entrancing.
See where they live — your enemies!
You cannot hope to fight them ...
Turn back your mind to delight, then,
In the harbour of my love.

Vieni a mirar la cerula
Marina tremolante;
Là Genova torreggia
Sul talamo spumante;
Là i tuoi nemici imperano,
Vincerli indarno speri ...
[10] Ripara i tuoi pensieri
Al porto dell'amor.

GABRIELE

Angel from the empyrean
You come to earth a stranger,
Showing a path of shining light
Through all our pain and anger.
Don't try to solve this mystery,
Hatred is here to spite you.
Turn back your mind to delight
In the harbour of my love.

Angiol che dall'empireo
Piegasti a terra l'ale,
E come faro sfolgori
Sul tramite mortale,
Non ricercar dell'odio
I funebri misteri;
Ripara i tuoi pensieri
Al porto dell'amor.

AMELIA
(*looking to the right*)

Ah!

Ah!

GABRIELE

What is it?

Che fia?

AMELIA

Do you see that man ... that seems
To appear every day?

Vedi là quell'uom? ... qual ombra
Ogni dì appar.

A maid enters.

53

GABRIELE

Maybe a rival? . . .   Forse un rival?

Scene Three. *The same, a maid, then Pietro.*

MAID

A messenger   Del Doge
Has come from the Doge.   Un messagger di te chiede.

AMELIA

Admit him.   S'appressi.

Exit the maid.

GABRIELE

I must see . . . who is it?   Chi sia veder vogl'io . . .
He is about to leave.

AMELIA
(*stopping him*)

Don't go now.   T'arresta.

PIETRO
(*Entering, he bows to Amelia and says:*)

The Doge   Il Doge
Is returning from hunting in Savona   Dalle caccie tornando di Savona
And he desires to see this mansion.   Questa magion visitar brama.

AMELIA

He may do so.   Il puote.

Pietro bows and leaves.

Scene Four. *Gabriele and Amelia.*

GABRIELE

The Doge is here?   Il Doge qui?

AMELIA

He comes to beg my hand.   Mia destra a chieder viene.

GABRIELE

For whom?   Per chi?

AMELIA

For someone who's his favourite. Go off   Pel favorito suo. D'Andrea
And find Andrea . . . But hurry now . . .   Vola in cerca . . . Affrettati . . . va . . .
Prepare   prepara
Our marriage today . . . Lead me to the   Il rito nuzial . . . mi guida all'ara.
altar.

AMELIA AND GABRIELE

Now let's rejoice in happiness,   [11] Sì, sì dell'ara il giubilo
Our fortune undivided;   Contrasti il fato avverso,
Whatever fate's decided   E tutto l'universo
I will defy with you.   Io sfiderò con te.

A force of love so passionate,   Innamorato anelito
That nothing can be stronger.   È del destin più forte;
The only thing I long for —   Amanti oltre la morte
All of my life with you.   Sempre vivrai con me.

Amelia enters the palace.

54

Scene Five. *Gabriele is about to leave to the right and meets Andrea.[2] / Scena and Duet.*

GABRIELE

(It's good I've found him!)   (Propizio ei giunge!)

ANDREA

You! You come here   Tu si mattutino
Very early! . . .   Qui! . . .

GABRIELE

To tell you . . .   A dirti . . .

ANDREA

You love Amelia.   Ch'ami Amelia.

GABRIELE

You always guard her with a father's   Tu che lei vegli con paterna cura
feeling,
Will you allow our marriage?   A nostre nozze assenti?

ANDREA

There is a mystery   Alto mistero
Hanging over Amelia.   Sulla vergine incombe.

GABRIELE

What's that?   E qual?

ANDREA

If I tell you,   Se parlo
Maybe your love would fade away.   Forse tu più non l'amerai.

GABRIELE

I love that girl   Non teme
And I fear no sort of mystery. I'll hear you!   Ombra d'arcani l'amor mio. T'ascolto!

ANDREA [3]

The girl you love is born of humble   Amelia tua d'umile stirpe nacque.
parents.

GABRIELE

The daughter of Grimaldi?   La figlia dei Grimaldi?

---

[2] The 1857 version of the duet ended with a brilliant cabaletta, a coda and a 'battery of chords followed by applause and curtain calls. No such good fortune for the singers in 1881; for as Amelia enters the palace the music moves to a half close in a new key.' (Budden, p. 294)

Scene Five. *Gabriele is about to leave, right, but meets Andrea.*

GABRIELE

(What luck — Andrea!)   (Propizio giunge Andrea!)

ANDREA

So early   Si mattutino
Here?   Qui?

---

[3] 1857:

ANDREA

If she were humbly born?   Se umil sua culla fosse?

GABRIELE

Humbly!! . . . a Grimaldi? . . .   Umile!! una Grimaldi? . . .

ANDREA

No — the daughter
Of Grimaldi was taken to a convent
And died there in Pisa. An orphan had
  been
Brought to the cloister that day, just as
  Amelia lay dying,
And she was given her cell . . .

No — la figlia
Dei Grimaldi morì tra consacrate
Vergini in Pisa. Un'orfana raccolta

Nel chiostro il dì che fu d'Amelia estremo

Ereditò sua cella . . .

GABRIELE

But why would the Grimaldi
Give their name to an orphan?

Ma come de' Grimaldi
Anco il nome prendea?

ANDREA

They were in exile
And the Doge had designs on their
  possessions;
But with the false Amelia he could not
Lay his greedy hands on their wealth.

De' fuorusciti
Perseguia le ricchezze il nuovo Doge;

E la mentita Amelia alla rapace
Man sottrarle potea.

GABRIELE

I love the orphan!

L'orfana adoro!

ANDREA

You're worthy of her!

Di lei sei degno!

GABRIELE

Then may we be united?

A me fia dunque unita?

ANDREA[4]

On earth and in heaven!

In terra e in ciel!

---

[4] In 1857 there was an impressive and 'savage outburst against the Doge'. Basevi described 'Paventa o perfido' as the weakest number in the score. (Budden p. 295)

ANDREA

[On earth and in Heaven.] — But love does
  not reduce
Your ardour for the people's cause.

In terra e in ciel. — Ma non rallenti amore

La foga in te de' cittadini affetti.

A trumpet sounds.

GABRIELE

The Doge is coming. — Let us go. —
  Although it is believed
You are no more, he may well see
Fiesco in Andrea . . .

Il doge vien — Partiam — Benchè la fatua

Ti dica estinto, ci ravvisar potria
Fiesco in Andrea . . .

ANDREA

The dreaded hour approaches;
Already the ominous plot,
Devised by the Guelphs for vengeance,
  awaits us.

S'appressa ora fatale;
Già noi de' Guelfi aspetta
Il convegno forier della vendetta.

GABRIELE

Fear, O treacherous
Doge, fear! . . .
I now avenge a father's
Bloody shade.

Paventa, o perfido
Doge, paventa! . . .
D'un padre io vendico
L'ombra cruenta.

ANDREA

Fear, O treacherous
Doge, fear! . . .

Paventa, o perfido
Doge, paventa! . . .

56

GABRIELE

You give me life now!   Mi dai la vita!

ANDREA

Come, my son, and kneel before me   [12] Vieni a me, ti benedico
In the calm of this great moment.   Nella pace di quest'ora,
Live in peace and faithfully love   Lieto vivi e fido adora
Your dear angel, your country, your God.   L'angiol tuo, la patria, il ciel!

GABRIELE

Now I feel the voice of an ancient time,   [13] Eco pia del tempo antico,
Now I can know this a holy enchantment;   La tua voce è un casto incanto;
All my life I will remember   Serberà ricordo santo
This the blessing you bestow.   Di quest'ora il cor fedel.

(*Trumpets sound offstage.*)

The Doge is here. Let's go. He must not see   Il Doge vien. Partiam. Ch'ei non ti scorga.
you.

ANDREA

Ah! May the day of my revenge come   Ah! presto il dì della vendetta sorga!
quickly!

They leave. Amelia, accompanied by several attendants, comes from the left. The Doge enters from the right with Paolo, followed by huntsmen.

Scene Six. / *Scene and Duet.*

DOGE

Paolo!   Paolo!

PAOLO

My lord!   Signor!

DOGE

      Events are very pressing,   Ci spronano gli eventi,
And we shall have to leave.   Di qua partir convien.

PAOLO

    When?   Quando?

DOGE

     On the stroke   Allo squillo
Of the hour.   Dell'ora.

PAOLO
(*catching sight of Amelia as he leaves*)

  (Oh, how superb!)   (Oh qual beltà!)

At a sign from the Doge, his procession withdraws, the attendants retire and Amelia is left alone with him.

Footnote [4] continued. The versions converge with 'Di qua partir convien.'

That daughter slain   Mi chiede vindice
Bids me to take revenge.   La figlia spenta.

Exeunt at the back.

Scene Six. *The sound of trumpets draws nearer until the Doge enters from the right followed by Paolo, Pietro, Huntsmen, Guards; Amelia enters from the left with some of her attendants.*

DOGE
(*to Paolo*)

The news of celebration   Il nuovo dì festivo
Requires the Doge's presence in the city.   Chiede presente alla cittad il doge. —
So we must leave here.   Di qua partir convien.

Scene Seven. *Amelia and the Doge.*

DOGE

Am I addressing
Amelia Grimaldi?

Favella il Doge
Ad Amelia Grimaldi?

AMELIA

That is the name they call me.

Cosi nomata io sono.

DOGE

And what of all your exiled brothers?
Have they no desire for their homeland?

E gli esuli fratelli tuoi non punge
Desio di patria?

AMELIA

It may be ... but ...

Possente ... ma ...

DOGE

I know it ...
The proud Grimaldi all disdain to beg me,
And this will be the answer from their
  Doge ...

Intendo ...
A me inchinarsi sdegnano i Grimaldi ...
Cosi risponde a tanto orgoglio il Doge ...

He hands her a document.

AMELIA
(*reading*)

A pardon! This is their pardon?

Che veggio! ... il lor perdono?

DOGE

It was your beauty earned them their
  forgiveness.
Tell me, you are so beautiful,
Why did you hide away here?
The world is full of lovely things —
I wonder if you miss them?
You blushed as you assented ...

E denno a te della clemenza il dono.

[14] Dinne, perchè in quest'eremo
Tanta beltà chiudesti?
Del mondo mai le fulgide
Lusinghe non piangesti?
Il tuo rossor mel dice ...

AMELIA

You're wrong there, I'm quite contented.

T'inganni, io son felice ...

DOGE

At such an age, a lover ...

Agli anni tuoi l'amore ...

AMELIA

Ah! My secret's discovered!
I love an angel spirit
Who returns my love with passion ...
But there's a villain wants my hand ...
He's after my possessions.

Ah! mi leggesti in core!
Amo uno spirto angelico
Che ardente mi riama ...
Ma di me acceso, un perfido,
L'or de' Grimaldi brama ...

DOGE

Paolo!

Paolo!

AMELIA

You named the coward! ... And since
  you seem
To feel such a pity for my lonely future,
I shall tell you the secret that surrounds me.
I am not a Grimaldi!

Quel vil nomasti! ... E poichè tanta
Pietà ti muove dei destini miei,
Vo' svelarti il segreto che m'ammanta ...
Non sono una Grimaldi!

DOGE

Oh, Heaven! ... How so?

Oh! ciel ... chi sei?

I was raised as a humble orphan In the modest house of a woman Who lived on a lonely sea-shore Near to Pisa ...	[15] Orfanella il tetto umile M'accogliea d'una meschina, Dove presso alla marina Sorge Pisa ...

DOGE

How can this be?   In Pisa tu?

AMELIA

But the pious aged woman Was the only help I was given; I provoked the disdain of Heaven, ah! She was taken away from me.	Grave d'anni quella pia Era solo a me sostegno; Io provai del ciel lo sdegno, ah! Involata ella mi fu.
I remember how she trembled As she handed me a picture, And she told me these were the features Of the mother I'd never known.	Colla tremula sua mano Pinta effigie mi porgea, Le sembianze esser dicea Della madre ignota a me.
Then she kissed me and she blessed me, And she raised her eyes in prayer ... Oh, how often then I cried, Oh, the echoes cried to me.	Mi baciò, mi benedisse, Levò al ciel, pregando, i rai ... Quante volte la chiamai, L'eco sol risposta die'.

DOGE
(to himself)

(Ah! If this hope now, merciful heaven, If the joy that smiles on my spirit, Prove an illusion, may I perish! May my phantom disappear!)	(Ah! Se la speme, o ciel clemente, Ch'or sorride all'alma mia, Fosse sogno! ... estinto io sia Della larva al disparir!)

AMELIA

Oh, how bitter in my sorrow Was the future then to me! Oh, how bitter!	Come tetro a me dolente S'appressava l'avvenir! [16] Come triste!

DOGE

Tell me. Was there someone you saw there?   Dinne ... alcun là non vedesti? ...

AMELIA

Yes, a seaman used to visit ...   Uom di mar noi visitava ...

DOGE

And would she be called Giovanna, The protector whom you lost?	E Giovanna si nomava Lei che i fati a te rapir?

AMELIA

Yes.   Si.

DOGE
(taking a portrait from his breast, handing it to Amelia who examines it)

Was the portrait anything like This one?	E l'effigie non somiglia Questa?

AMELIA

It's just the same!   Uguali son! ...

DOGE

Maria!   Maria!

AMELIA

My name's Maria!   Il nome mio! ...

DOGE

You're my daughter!   Sei mia figlia!

AMELIA

Daughter ...   Io ...

DOGE

   Embrace me, o my daughter!   M'abbraccia, o figlia mia.

AMELIA

Father!   Padre!

DOGE

Ah! Daughter, daughter! How you move   Ah! figlia, il cor ti chiama!
me!

AMELIA

Ah! Hold her close, Maria who loves you!   Ah! Stringi al sen Maria che t'ama.

DOGE

Daughter! My heart leaps at the word!   [17] Figlia! . . . a tal nome palpito
I see the heavens open . . .   Qual se m'aprisse i cieli . . .
I see amazing happiness   Un mondo d'ineffabili
In all the truth you show me.   Letizie a me riveli;
Now let your father offer you   Un paradiso il tenero[5]
Riches and great renown.   Padre ti schiuderà . . .
You are my greatest blessing,   Di mia corona il raggio
The glory of my crown.   La gloria tua sarà.

AMELIA

Father, you'll see me always there,   [18] Padre, vedrai la vigile
I will be there beside you.   Figlia a te sempre accanto;
When darkness weighs upon your soul   Nell'ora me malinconica
I will be there to guide you.   Asciugherò il tuo pianto . . .
And we will be so happy,   Avrem gioie romite[5]
And there will be such love.   Soltanto note al ciel,
In your royal palace   Io la colomba mite
I'll be your tender dove.   Sarò del regio ostel.

They embrace. Then Amelia, accompanied by her father to the threshold, enters the palace.

DOGE
(watching ecstatically, as she leaves, says for the last time:)

Daughter!   Figlia!

---

* The duet, in the 1857 version, ended with an 'orthodox' cabaletta. (Budden p. 300)

DOGE

[Now let your father offer you   Qui un paradiso il tenero
Riches and great renown]   Padre ti schiuderà . . .
In my crown, the radiance   Di mia corona il raggio
You will be.   Aureola tua sarà.

AMELIA

Not with the fleeting glory   Non di regale orgoglio
Of regal splendour,   L'effimero splendor,
You will encircle me   Mi cingerà d'aureola
With the radiance of love.   Il raggio dell' amor.

DOGE

Such tender feelings for me, target that I   Ma sì teneri affetti a me, bersaglio
am
For patrician hatred, may not be shown.   A patrizio livor, mostrar non lice.

AMELIA

Yet I will live happy with this secret.   Io nel mistero ancor vivrò felice.

Accompanied by the Doge as far as the doorway, she goes into the room on the left.

Scene Eight. *The Doge, Paolo approaches hurriedly from the right.*

PAOLO

What did she say?   Che rispose?

DOGE

Give up all hope of marriage.   Rinunzia a ogni speranza.

PAOLO

Doge, I cannot!   Doge, nol posso!

DOGE

I wish it.   Il voglio.

Exit the Doge to the right.

PAOLO

You wish! . . . You wish! Have you   Il vuoi! . . . scordasti che mi devi il soglio?
forgotten what you owe me?

Scene Nine. *Paolo, and Pietro from the right.*

PIETRO

The answer?   Che disse?

PAOLO

He has refused me.   A me negolla.

PIETRO

What do we do?   Che pensi tu?

PAOLO

We take her.   Rapirla.

PIETRO

Take her?   Come?

PAOLO

She walks the beach   Sul lido a sera
Every evening unattended . . .   La troverai solinga . . .
You take her to my vessel;   Si tragga al mio naviglio;
From there you hand her over   Di Lorenzin si rechi
To Lorenzin.   Alla magion.

PIETRO

He's with you?   S'ei nega?

PAOLO

You tell him I know the plot he's made   Digli che so sue trame,
And he will lend assistance . . .   E presterammi aita . . .
You, I'll pay you well in gold.   Tu gran mercede avrai.

PIETRO

Well then, the woman will be taken.   Ella, ella sarà rapita.

Exeunt.

Scene Ten.[6] *The Council Chamber in the Doge's Palace.*
The Doge is seated on the ducal throne; on one side twelve councillors from the nobles; on the other twelve councillors from the people. Seated separately are four maritime consuls and the constables. Paolo and Pietro are on the back benches of the people's party. A herald. / First finale. [19]

<table>
<tr><td colspan="2" align="center">DOGE</td></tr>
<tr>
<td>My council, the noble king of Tartary
Has sent you pledges of peace and costly gifts,
And announces that the Black Sea welcomes the ships of Liguria.
Do you accept this?</td>
<td>Messeri, il re di Tartaria vi porge
Pegni di pace e ricchi doni e annuncia
Schiuso l'Eusin alle liguri prore.

Acconsentite?</td>
</tr>
</table>

<table>
<tr><td colspan="2" align="center">COUNCILLORS</td></tr>
<tr>
<td align="center">Yes.</td>
<td align="center">Sì.</td>
</tr>
</table>

<table>
<tr><td colspan="2" align="center">DOGE</td></tr>
<tr>
<td align="center">And now I request
Another, more generous, decision.</td>
<td align="center">Ma d'altro voto
Più generoso io vi richiedo.</td>
</tr>
</table>

<table>
<tr><td colspan="2" align="center">COUNCILLORS</td></tr>
<tr>
<td align="center">Tell us.</td>
<td align="center">Parla.</td>
</tr>
</table>

<table>
<tr><td colspan="2" align="center">DOGE</td></tr>
<tr>
<td>The very voice which thundered once on Rienzi,
With a prophecy of glory and his destruction,
Thunders now over Genoa. Here is a message</td>
<td>La stessa voce che tuonò su Rienzi,
Vaticinio di gloria e poi di morte
Or su Genova tuona. — Ecco un messaggio</td>
</tr>
</table>

(holding up a letter)

<table>
<tr>
<td>From the hermit of Sorga. He is requesting
Peace for the Venetians . . .</td>
<td>Del romito di Sorga; ei per Venezia
Supplica pace . . .</td>
</tr>
</table>

<table>
<tr><td colspan="2" align="center">PAOLO
(interrupting)</td></tr>
<tr>
<td align="center">Let Petrarch stick to his poems
And sing of the beauty of his fair girl.</td>
<td align="center">Attenda alle sue rime
Il cantor della bionda Avignonese.</td>
</tr>
</table>

<table>
<tr><td colspan="2" align="center">COUNCILLORS
(fiercely)</td></tr>
<tr>
<td>War now with Venice!</td>
<td>Guerra a Venezia!</td>
</tr>
</table>

<table>
<tr><td colspan="2" align="center">DOGE</td></tr>
<tr>
<td>With such a hideous shout
Between the two shores of Italy
Cain lifts a club soaked with the blood of our people!
Adria and Liguria have a homeland in common.</td>
<td>E con quest'urlo atroce
Fra due liti d'Italia erge Caino
La sua clava cruenta! — Adria e Liguria
Hanno patria comune.</td>
</tr>
</table>

<table>
<tr><td colspan="2" align="center">COUNCILLORS</td></tr>
<tr>
<td>It's our homeland,
Genoa.</td>
<td align="right">È nostra patria
Genova.</td>
</tr>
</table>

There is a very distant offstage noise of a crowd. [20a] *Paolo leaps to the balcony.*

<table>
<tr><td colspan="2" align="center">PIETRO</td></tr>
<tr>
<td>What's that shout?</td>
<td>Qual clamor!</td>
</tr>
</table>

---

[6] This whole scene was added in 1880 to replace the 1857 scene which may be found on page 88.

COUNCILLORS

Where is that noise from?   D'onde tai grida?

PAOLO

From the piazza dei Fieschi.   Dalla piazza dei Fieschi.

COUNCILLORS
(getting to their feet)

It's a rebellion!   Una sommossa!

The noise of the crowd approaches.

PAOLO
(still at the window, where Pietro has joined him)

See! There's a crowd of people fleeing.   Ecco una turba di fuggenti.

DOGE

But listen.   Ascolta!

PAOLO
(listening)

I cannot catch a word ...   Si sperdon le parole ...

THE CROWD

Kill him! Kill him!   Morte! Morte!

PAOLO
(to Pietro)

It's him.   È lui?

DOGE
(hearing this)

Who?   Chi?

PIETRO

Look.   Guarda.

DOGE
(looking)

Heavens! Gabriele Adorno   Ciel! Gabriele Adorno
Is pursued by the rabble ... and at his side   Dalla plebe inseguito ... accanto ad esso
There's a noble fighting. Send me a herald.   Combatte un Guelfo. A me un araldo.

PIETRO
(quietly)

       Paolo,   Paolo,
Flee or you're done for.   Fuggi o sei colto.

DOGE
(watching Paolo leave)

       Consuls of the Sea,   Consoli del mare,
Make sure that all doors are guarded!   Custodite le soglie! Olà, chi fugge
   You hear!
It's treachery to flee.   È un traditor.

Paolo stops, confused.

THE CROWD
(offstage)

Death to the nobles!   Morte ai patrizi!

NOBLE COUNCILLORS
(drawing their swords)

To battle!   All'armi!

THE CROWD
(*offstage*)

Long live the people's cause!	Viva il popolo!

COUNCILLORS OF THE PEOPLE
(*drawing their swords*)

The people!	Evviva!

DOGE

What's that? You also?	E che? voi pure?
You, here!! Is this a challenge?	Voi, qui!! vi provocate?

THE CROWD
(*offstage*)

Death to the Doge!	Morte al Doge!

DOGE
(*proudly*)

Death to the Doge? Very well.	Morte al Doge? Sta ben!

(*to the herald*)

You, herald, open	Tu, araldo, schiudi
The gates of the palace . . . tell the crowd	Le porte del palagio e annuncia al volgo
Of nobles and plebeians I do not fear them,	Gentilesco e plebeo ch'io non lo temo,
That I have heard their threats . . . here I await them.	Che le minaccie udii, che qui li attendo . . .

(*to the Councillors, who obey*)

Now take your swords and sheathe them.	Nelle guaine i brandi.

THE CROWD
(*offstage*)

Battle and plunder!	[20b] Armi! saccheggio!
Burn all the houses!	Fuoco alle case!
To the gallows!	Ai trabocchi!
To the pillory!	Alla gogna!

A long trumpet blast.

DOGE

Now comes the trumpet of the herald. He's speaking . . .	Squilla la tromba del'araldo . . . ei parla . . .

Everyone stands listening. Silence.

All now is silent.	Tutto è silenzio . . .

A VOICE FROM THE CROWD

Evviva!	Evviva!

THE CROWD
(*approaching, still offstage*)

Evviva Simone!	Evviva il Doge!

DOGE

Here comes the rabble!	Ecco le plebi!

Scene Eleven. *The crowd bursts in — men (plebeians), women and children, etc.. They drag in Adorno and Fiesco.*

THE CROWD

For vengeance! For vengeance!	Vendetta! Vendetta!
Blood calls out for vengeance!	Spargarsi il sangue del fiero uccisor!
Kill the murdering lord! The man must be killed!	Spargarsi il sangue del fiero uccisor!

DOGE
(*ironically*)

Is this really the voice of all the people?	Quest'è dunque del popolo la voce?

64

From the distance a hurricane in spate, but closer
A cry of women, a shout of children. Adorno,
Why's your sword in your hand?

Da lungi tuono d'uragan, da presso
Grido di donne e di fanciulli. — Adorno
Perchè impugni l'acciar?

GABRIELE

I've killed the villain Lorenzino.

Ho trucidato Lorenzino.

THE CROWD

You shall die!

Assassin!

GABRIELE

He was abducting Young Amelia.

Ei la Grimaldi Aveva rapita.

DOGE
(aside)

(Oh no!)

(Orror!)

THE CROWD

Liar!

GABRIELE

That coward,
Before he died, said he was hired to do the crime
By a man of power.

Quel vile
Pria di morir disse che un uom possente
Al crimine l'ha spinto.

PIETRO
(to Paolo)

(Ah, you're discovered!)

(Ah! sei scoperto!)

DOGE
(anxiously)

What was his name?

E il nome suo?

GABRIELE
(staring at the Doge with deep irony)

Rest easy! The man was dying! He never told me.

T'acqueta! il reo si spense Pria di svelarlo.

DOGE

What do you mean?

Che vuoi dir?

GABRIELE
(with terrible ferocity)

By heaven! All the power lies with you!

Pel cielo! Uom possente se' tu!

DOGE
(to Gabriele)

How dare you!

Ribaldo!

GABRIELE
(threatening the Doge)

You villainous Abductor of women!

Audace Rapitor di fanciulle!

THE COUNCILLORS

Disarm him!

Si disarmi!

GABRIELE
(freeing himself as though about to strike the Doge)

Murdering corsair with a crown! Die!   Empio corsaro incoronato! muori!

Scene Twelve. *The aforesaid, with Amelia.*

AMELIA
(rushing between Gabriele and the Doge)

Then kill me!   Ferisci!

DOGE, FIESCO, GABRIELE

Amelia!   Amelia!

THE COUNCILLORS AND THE CROWD

Amelia!   Amelia!

AMELIA

O Doge . . . ah, save him . . .   O Doge . . . ah salva . . .
Save him, my lord, I beg.   Salva l'Adorno tu.

DOGE
(to the guards who have seized Gabriele to disarm him)

Let no-one harm him.   Nessun l'offenda.
Pride has subsided. The sound of sorrow   Cade l'orgoglio e al suon del suo dolore
Speaks to my affection and says: do what Tutta l'anima mia parla d'amore . . .
  she asks you . . .
Amelia, say how you came to be captured   Amelia, di' come fosti rapita
And how you were able to flee from the   E come al periglio potesti scampar.
  danger.

AMELIA

The evening was falling, the air was   [21] Nell'ora soave che all'estasi invita
  enchanting.
I went for a walk by the shore of the sea. Soletta men givo sul lido del mar.
Three ruffians took hold of me; a ship lay Mi cingon tre sgherri, m'accoglie un
  in waiting.   naviglio.
I was suffocating and I could not shout.   Soffocati non valsero i gridi . . .
I fainted and the next I knew, when I   Io svenni al novello dischiuder del ciglio
  recovered,
I found I'd been taken to the house of   Lorenzo in sue stanze presente mi vidi . . .
  Lorenzo.

ALL

Lorenzo!   Lorenzo!

AMELIA

And I was his captive — I saw I was   Mi vidi prigion dell'infame!
  the
Villain's captive. I already knew what a   Io ben di quell'alma sapea la viltà.
  coward he was.
Simone, I told him, knows all that you're   Al Doge, gli dissi, fien note tue trame,
  plotting.
Release me this instant or hope for the   Se a me sull'istante non dai libertà.
  worst.
He started in terror and quickly released   Confuso di tema, mi schiuse le porte . . .
  me.
The threat was enough then to save me   Salvarmi l'audace minaccia potea . . .
  from worse.

ALL

The villain! He richly deserved what he   Ei ben meritava, quell'empio, la morte.
  suffered.

AMELIA

There's someone more evil who's still
going free.

V'è un più nefando che illeso ancor sta.

ALL

Who is it?

Chi dunque?

AMELIA

He can hear me. I see now his lips
Have grown ashen.

Ei m'ascolta ... discerno le smorte
Sue labbra.

GABRIELE, DOGE

Who is it?

Chi dunque?

THE CROWD
(threatening)

A patrician.

Un patrizio.

NOBLES
(threatening)

A plebeian.

Un plebeo.

THE CROWD
(to the nobles)

Away with the nobles!

Abbasso le spade!

AMELIA

What terror is threatened?

Terribili gridi!

NOBLES
(to the crowd)

Away with the rabble!

Abbasso le scuri!

AMELIA

No more!

Pietà!

DOGE
(with all his might)

Murdering brothers!!!

Fratricidi!!!

People! Patricians! Progeny
Of a ferocious history,
Inheritors of hatred
Of the Spinola and Doria.
Broad though the ocean's empire lies,
Calling for deeds of heroes,
You must prefer your squabbles —
You tear yourselves apart.

[22] Plebe! Patrizi! — Popolo
Dalla feroce storia!
Erede sol dell'odio
Dei Spinola, dei Doria,
Mentre v'invita estatico
Il regno ampio dei mari,
Voi nei fraterni lari
Vi lacerate il cor.

I weep for you. The sun is so
Gentle upon your hillsides.
Vainly the flowers blossom,
Vainly the fruits are spilling.
I weep. In vain the olive
Swells in the silver groves.
All that I ask is peace, now!
All that I ask is love!

Piango su voi, sul placido
Raggio del vostro clivo
Là dove invan germoglia
Il ramo dell'ulivo.
Piango sulla mendace
Festa dei vostri fior,
[23] E vo gridando: pace!
E vo gridando: amor!

THE COUNCILLORS AND THE CROWD
(their eyes turned to the Doge)

See how his words are moving
To make our anger calm,
Like gentle breezes blowing
After the thunderstorm.

Il suo commosso accento
Sa l'ira in noi calmar;
Vol di soave vento
Che rasserena il mar.

67

AMELIA
(to Fiesco)

(Calm now! Oh, let me beg you,
Give up your fierce disdain,
Calm now! Oh, feel it — a sense of,
A love of, fatherland.)

[24] (Pace! lo sdegno immenso
Nascondi per pietà!
Pace! t'ispiri un senso
Di patria carità.)

GABRIELE

(Amelia is safe! She loves me!
Oh, thank the Lord of Heaven!
All other strong desires
Are far from my faithful heart.)

(Amelia è salva, e m'ama!
Sia ringraziato il ciel!
Disdegna ogn'altra brama
L'animo mio fedel.)

FIESCO

(What can my country hope for?
A life of shame and misery.
See how the city languishes
Within a pirate's fist.)

(O patria! A qual mi serba
Vergogna il mio sperar!
Sta la città superba
Nel pugno d'un corsar!)

PIETRO
(to Paolo)

(Everything's lost! Escape then!
Look to your safety now!)

(Tutto fallì, la fuga
Sia tua salvezza almen.)

PAOLO
(to Pietro)

(No — I am filled with poison.
My revenge is due.)

(No, l'angue che mi fruga
Gonfio è di velen.)

GABRIELE
(giving up his sword to the Doge)

Here, take my sword.

Ecco la spada.

DOGE

For tonight you will be prisoner here,
Until the plot has been discovered.
No, you keep your noble weapon.
I need no more than your assurance.

Questa notte
Prigione sarai, finchè la trama
Tutta si scopra. — No, l'altera lama
Serba, non voglio che la tua parola.

GABRIELE

You have it!

E sia!

DOGE
(with terrible authority)

Paolo!

Paolo!

PAOLO
(emerging from the crowd in confusion)

My master!

Mio Duce!

[25]

DOGE
(with awe inspiring majesty and ever increasing ferocity)

In you is vested
The majesty of the people's law; your
loyalty
Is a guarantee for all the city,
I need some help from you ... within this
palace a coward
Hates me, and now his face grows pale.
Here is my hand: already I can reach him.
I know his name ...
I know the fear he suffers.
You, in the sight of all Heaven and in my
sight,

In te risiede
L'austero dritto popolar, è accolto
L'onore cittadin nella tua fede:
Bramo l'ausilio tuo ... V'è in queste
mura
Un vil che m'ode e impallidisce in volto,
Già la mia man l'afferra per le chiome.
Io so il suo nome ...
È nella sua paura.
Tu al cospetto del ciel e al mio cospetto

68

Bear witness with me. Now on the villain's head	Sei testimon. — Sul manigoldo impuro
Let my curse fall like thunder:	Piombi il tuon del mio detto:
He's cursed for ever!	[26] *Sia maledetto!*

(darkly and terribly to Paolo)

Now you repeat the oath.	E tu ripeti il giuro.

PAOLO

(*terrified and trembling*)

He's cursed for ever ... (Oh, horror!)	*Sia maledetto ... (Orrore!)*

ALL THE OTHERS

He's cursed for ever!!	*Sia maledetto!!*

Everyone gradually disperses, repeating the curse.

PAOLO

(Oh, no!)	(Orror!)

He runs off.

The Council Chamber scene at the Met., 1984 (photo: James Heffernan)

69

Act Two

The Doge's room in the Ducal Palace in Genoa.
Doors on each side. The city is visible from the balcony. A table, a jug and a goblet. Night is drawing in.

Scene One. *Paolo and Pietro / Scene and Duet.*

PAOLO
(to Pietro, drawing him towards the balcony)

You saw those people?   Quei due vedesti?

PIETRO

Yes.   Sì.

PAOLO

Then bring them quickly   Li traggi tosto
From prison, using the secret approach   Dal carcer loro per l'andito ascoso,
Which this set of keys will unlock.   Che questa chiave schiuderà.

PIETRO

I'll do it.   T'intesi.

He leaves.

Scene Two.[7] *Paolo alone.*

PAOLO

The victim of my own curse!   Me stesso ho maledetto!
And it's a curse   E l'anatèma
That pursues me still ... the very air still   M'insegue ancor ... e l'aura ancor ne
   trembles!   trema!
They despise me, reject me,   Vilipeso ... reietto
In the Senate, in Genoa. So here   Dal Senato, da Genova, qui vibro
I string my last arrow before my flight. I   L'ultimo stral prima di fuggir, qui libro
   measure
What your fate will be, Simone, in this   La sorte tua, Doge, in quest'ansia estrema.
   moment of anguish.
You dared defy me though you owed me   Tu, che m'offendi e che mi devi il trono,
   your fortune.
Here I abandon you   Qui t'abbandono
To your destiny.   Al tuo destino
Now your doom is upon you.   In quest'ora fatale ...
          (He takes out a phial and pours the contents into the goblet.)
I here prepare you a long and painful   Qui ti stillo una lenta, atra agonia ...
   torment.
There, there is your assassin.   Là t'armo un assassino.
Now let death choose his weapon: Scelga morte sua via
The poison or the dagger.   Fra il tosco ed il pugnale.

---

[7] In 1857, Paolo's soliloquy was shorter. See Budden p. 316 (*op. cit.*)

Scene Two.

PAOLO
(alone)

O ungrateful Doge! ... That I must give   O Doge ingrato! ... ch'io rinunci Amelia
   up Amelia
And her charms? ... in three days, exile   E i suoi tesori? ... fra tre dì a me il bando?
For me, to whom you owe the throne.   A me cui devi il trono.
Three days are too many for revenge on   Tre giorni troppi alla vendetta sono.
   you.

Scene Three. *Paolo, Fiesco and Gabriele led by Pietro, who then withdraws.*

FIESCO

Tell me, where are you leading me prisoner? [27]   Prigioniero in qual loco m'adduci?

PAOLO

To the Doge's apartment. And it's Paolo   Nelle stanze del Doge, e favella
Who's speaking.   A te Paolo.

FIESCO[8]

In your looks there is murder.   I tuoi sguardi son truci . . .

PAOLO

I'm aware of the hatred in you.   Io so l'odio che celasi in te.
You must hear me.   Tu m'ascolta.

FIESCO

Why should I?   Che brami?

PAOLO

You have organised   Al cimento
A band of the Guelphs for rebellion?   Preparasti de' Guelfi la schiera?

FIESCO

Yes . . .   Sì . . .

PAOLO

But things can go wrong with   Ma vano fia tanto ardimento!
rebellion.
For this Doge, I despise and abhor him   Questo Doge, abborrito da me
As deeply as you do. He's planning   Quanto voi l'abborrite, v'appresta
Now to thwart you.   Nuovo scempio . . .

FIESCO

You're hoping to trap me.   Mi tendi un agguato.

PAOLO

Why to trap you? The sentence of Fiesco —   Un agguato? . . . Di Fiesco la testa
Has the tyrant not signed it already?   Il tiranno segnata non ha? . . .
I will teach you to triumph.   Io t'insegno vittoria.

FIESCO

By what method?   A qual patto?

PAOLO

You could kill him here, while he is   Trucidarlo qui, mentre egli dorme . . .
sleeping . . .

FIESCO

Do you dare to suggest such dishonour?   Osi a Fiesco proporre un misfatto?

---

[8] The 1857 version of this scene retains the reference to Fiesco's alias, and converges on the
line 'Al cimento'.

FIESCO

That name is new to me.   Tal nome m'è nuovo.

PAOLO

I know the name you hide within yourself.   Io so il nome che celasi in te.
You are Fiesco.   Tu sei Fiesco.

FIESCO

What are you talking about?   Che parli? . . .

71

PAOLO

You refuse me?   Tu rifiuti?

FIESCO

   Yes.   Sì.

PAOLO[9]

   Then return to your cell.   Al carcer ten va.

Exit Fiesco. Gabriele makes after him but is stopped by Paolo.

Scene Four. *Paolo and Gabriele. / Scene and Aria.*

PAOLO

You heard that?   Udisti?

GABRIELE

   Loathsome coward!   Vil disegno!

PAOLO

So you have never loved the young Amelia?   Amelia dunque mai tu non amasti?

GABRIELE

What's that?   Che dici?

PAOLO

   She's here.   È qui.

GABRIELE

   Not Amelia!   Qui Amelia!

PAOLO

    And she's intended   E del vegliardo
Now for the old man's foulest pleasures.   Segno è alle infami dilettanze.

GABRIELE

   Insidious   Astuto
Fiend, silence . . .   Dimon, cessa . . .
(Paolo hastens to close the door on the right.)
   What's that?   Che fai?

PAOLO

I've locked every door into this chamber.   Da qui ogni varco t'è conteso — Ardisci
  Now dare
To kill him. Or you will   Il colpo . . . O sepoltura
Meet your death within this palace.   Avrai fra queste mura.

Exit hurriedly by the door on the left, which shuts behind him.

Scene Five. *Gabriele alone.*

GABRIELE

You devil! Amelia here? Here with the old   O inferno! . . . Amelia qui? . . . L'ama il
  man?   vegliardo!
All the anger within me   E il furor che m'accende
Will be bound to burst forth. You murdered   M'è conteso sfogar! . . . Tu m'uccidesti
My dear father. You have stolen my beloved. Il padre . . . tu m'involi il mio tesoro . . .

---

[9] In the 1857 version the scene ends:

PAOLO

Simpleton! — Go!   Stolido. — Va.

Exit Fiesco right; Gabriele goes to follow him but is stopped by Paolo.

72

You shall tremble. The first offence was sufficient.	Trema, iniquo . . . già troppa era un'offesa,
But now the second! Now for a double vengeance!	Doppia vendetta hai sul tuo capo accesa!

Ah, see how a burning jealousy [28]	Sento avvampar nell'anima
Has set my senses reeling!	Furente gelosia;
All of my blood wouldn't quench the blazing	Tutto il mio sangue spegnere
Fire of my dark feelings.	L'incendio non potria;
If he was mine to murder,	S'ei mille vite avesse,
With a thousand necks to proffer —	E spegnerle potesse
One blow would cut them off . . .	D'un colpo il mio furor,
No! That would not sate me,	No, non sarei sazio ancor,
That would not sate my wrath.	Non sarei sazio ancor.

Ah! What's this? . . . Alas! . . . It's madness!	Che parlo! . . . Ahimè! . . . Deliro . . .
I'm weeping! . . . O God have pity, pity me in all my torment!	Io piango! . . . pietà, gran Dio, del mio martiro!

Come now, my love, come back to me. [29]	Cielo pietoso, rendila,
Come to me and I shall know you.	Rendila a questo core,
Spotless and pure as angels are,	Pura siccome l'angelo
As angels are watching over.	Che veglia al suo pudore;
But if there's one suspicion,	Ma se una nube impura
One reason for contrition,	Tanto candor m'oscura,
If you're no longer true,	Priva di sue virtù,
Let me not gaze on you.	Ch'io non la vegga più.

Scene Six. *Gabriele and Amelia.*

AMELIA

It's you.	Tu qui? . . .

GABRIELE

Amelia!	Amelia!

AMELIA

Who let you come in here?	Chi il varco t'apria?

GABRIELE

And you . . . what of you?	E tu come qui?

AMELIA

Me?	Io?

GABRIELE

Disloyal!	Sleale!

AMELIA

Oh, that's cruel!	Oh crudele! . . .

GABRIELE

And that monster the tyrant . . .	Il tiranno ferale . . .

AMELIA

You should love him . . .	Il rispetta . . .

GABRIELE

Does he love you?	Egli t'ama . . .

AMELIA

With a pure love.	D'amor Santo . . .

GABRIELE

And you?	E tu? . . .

73

AMELIA

I love him also.   L'amo del pari . . .

GABRIELE

And I hear   E t'ascolto,
But do not kill you.   E non t'uccido?

AMELIA

Gabriele, believe me,   Infelice! . . . mel credi,
I am pure.   Pura io son . . .

GABRIELE

You're lying.   Favella . . .

AMELIA

Believe me,   Concedi
Just a while. I cannot yet explain.   Che il segreto non aprasi ancor.

GABRIELE

Give me a reason why I should   [30] Parla, in tùo cor virgineo
Believe you do not hate me.   Fede al diletto rendi.
If you keep silent I feel I'm dying,   Il tuo silenzio è funebre
I'm dying — the grave awaits me.   Vel che su me distendi.
Give me a reason not to die,   Dammi la vita o il feretro,
Do not have pity on me.   Sdegno la tua pietà.

AMELIA

Oh, do not doubt I'm faithful.   Sgombra dall'alma il dubbio . . .
Deep in my heart I cherish   Santa nel petto mio
An image of you so holy   L'immagin tua s'accoglie
Such as will never perish.   Quale nel tempio Iddìo.
No stormy shadow clouds the sky.   No, procellosa tenebra
You stand alone for me.   Un ciel d'amor non ha.

(A trumpet fanfare is heard.)

The Doge is here. There's no escape. Go   Il Doge vien. Scampo non hai.
   hide yourself.   T'ascondi!

GABRIELE

No.   No.

AMELIA

You are marked for the gallows.   Il patibol t'aspetta.

GABRIELE

I do not fear them.   Io non lo temo.

AMELIA

We die together this very moment   All'ora i stessa teco avrò morte . . .
Unless you promise to pity me.   Se non ti move di me pietà.

GABRIELE

You ask for pity?   Di te pietade?
               (aside)
(Now comes the moment.   (Lo vuol la sorte . . .
The man is fated. It has to be.)   Si compia il fato . . . Egli morrà . . .)

AMELIA

He's coming. I'll hide you.   Ei viene . . . T'ascondi . . .

She hides Gabriele on the balcony.

Scene Seven. *The Doge enters reading a document. / Scene and Terzetto — Second Finale*

DOGE

Daughter!   Figlia!

74

<table>
<tr><td colspan="2" align="center">AMELIA</td></tr>
<tr><td>O father, you are troubled.</td><td>Sì afflitto, o padre mio?</td></tr>
</table>

<table>
<tr><td colspan="2" align="center">DOGE</td></tr>
<tr><td>That's not so.
But you've been crying.</td><td>T'inganni...
Ma tu piangevi.</td></tr>
</table>

<table>
<tr><td colspan="2" align="center">AMELIA</td></tr>
<tr><td>Crying?</td><td>Io?...</td></tr>
</table>

<table>
<tr><td colspan="2" align="center">DOGE</td></tr>
<tr><td>And I know the reason
For the tears you've been shedding. It's as
you told me ...
In love. Come tell me if the man
That you love is worthy of the honour.</td><td>La cagion m'è nota
Delle lagrime tue... Già mel dicesti...

Ami; or bene, s'è degno
Di te l'eletto del tuo core ...</td></tr>
</table>

<table>
<tr><td colspan="2" align="center">AMELIA</td></tr>
<tr><td>O father,
The finest of our people and the most noble.</td><td>O padre,
Fra' i Liguri il più prode, il più gentile.</td></tr>
</table>

<table>
<tr><td colspan="2" align="center">DOGE</td></tr>
<tr><td>Then tell me.</td><td>Il noma.</td></tr>
</table>

<table>
<tr><td colspan="2" align="center">AMELIA</td></tr>
<tr><td>Adorno ...</td><td>Adorno ...</td></tr>
</table>

<table>
<tr><td colspan="2" align="center">DOGE</td></tr>
<tr><td>But he's my enemy!</td><td>Il mio nemico!</td></tr>
</table>

<table>
<tr><td colspan="2" align="center">AMELIA</td></tr>
<tr><td>Father!</td><td>Padre!</td></tr>
</table>

<table>
<tr><td colspan="2" align="center">DOGE</td></tr>
<tr><td>See here — a list of all the traitors. He's
plotting
With the Guelphs ...</td><td>Vedi: qui scritto il nome suo?... congiura

Coi Guelfi ...</td></tr>
</table>

<table>
<tr><td colspan="2" align="center">AMELIA</td></tr>
<tr><td>Heaven! But pardon him!</td><td>Ciel!... perdonagli!</td></tr>
</table>

<table>
<tr><td colspan="2" align="center">DOGE</td></tr>
<tr><td>I cannot.</td><td>Nol posso.</td></tr>
</table>

<table>
<tr><td colspan="2" align="center">AMELIA</td></tr>
<tr><td>I'll die with him ...</td><td>Con lui morrò ...</td></tr>
</table>

<table>
<tr><td colspan="2" align="center">DOGE</td></tr>
<tr><td>You love him so much?</td><td>L'ami cotanto?</td></tr>
</table>

<table>
<tr><td colspan="2" align="center">AMELIA</td></tr>
<tr><td>My heart is
Burning with an infinite love. Either let us
At once be married, or suffer the
headman's axe
To despatch us both together ...</td><td>L'amo
D'ardente, d'infinito amor.[10] O al tempio
Con lui mi guida, o sovra entrambi cada

La scure del carnefice ...</td></tr>
</table>

---

[10] In the 1857 libretto:

<table>
<tr><td colspan="2" align="center">AMELIA</td></tr>
<tr><td>I love him
With a pure, inextinguishable flame.</td><td>Io l'amo
Di pura inestinguibil fiamma.</td></tr>
</table>

DOGE
(*in despair*)

How my destiny's
Cruel! All of my hopes are now in ruins!
Though I got back my daughter, I have lost
her to
My enemy. Now listen . . .
If he repented . . .

O crudele
Destino! O dileguate mie speranze!
Una figlia ritrovo; ed un nemico
A me la invola . . . Ascolta;
S'ei ravveduto . . .

AMELIA

He must do so.

Il fia . . .

DOGE

Then maybe I'd
Forgive . . .

Forse il perdono
Allor . . .

AMELIA

Ah, dearest father!

Padre adorato!

DOGE

You go off now.
I must await the dawn alone here.

Ti ritraggi . . .
Attender qui degg'io l'aurora . . .

AMELIA

Just let me
Stay here beside you.

Lascia
Ch'io vegli al tuo fianco . . .

DOGE

No, you go off now.

No, ti ritraggi . . .

AMELIA

Father!

Padre!

DOGE

I wish it.

Il voglio . . .

AMELIA
(*leaving to the left*)

(Oh God, how can I save him?)

(Gran Dio, come salvarlo?)

Scene Eight. *The Doge, and Adorno hidden.*

DOGE

Doge! Yet still all these traitors test your
clemency
Toward them. But if I were harsh
They would think me fearful. Oh, my
throat is burning —

Doge! ancor proveran la tua clemenza
I traditori? — Di paura segno
Fora il castigo. — M'ardono le fauci.

(*He pours from the jug into the goblet and drinks.*)

Even water from the spring tastes bitter
placed
On the lips of a ruler. Oh grief . . . My mind
is burdened.
My limbs are heavy. Alas — I must sleep a
little.

Perfin l'acqua del fonte è amara al labbro
Dell'uom che regna . . . O duol . . . la
mentè è oppressa . . .
Stanche le membra . . . ohimè! . . . mi
vince il sonno.

(*sitting*)

O Amelia, you are in love with my enemy . . .

Oh! Amelia . . . ami . . . un nemico . . .

He falls asleep. Gabriele enters cautiously, approaches the Doge and watches him.

GABRIELE

He's sleeping! Now what
Stops me from striking? Can it be fear or
reverence?

Ei dorme! . . . quale
Sento ritegno? . . . È reverenza o tema? . . .

76

James Johnston as Gabriele and Arnold Matters as Boccanegra, Sadler's Wells, in the 1948 British première (photo: Angus McBean © Harvard Theatre Collection)

Or is my will not strong? Old man, you're sleeping.	Vacilla il mio voler?
The man who killed my father. My rival too.	Del padre mio carnefice, tu mio
Son of Adorno! Now your father's shade Calls to you for vengeance.	Rival . . . Figlio d'Adorno! la paterna Ombra ti chiama vindice . . .

He draws a dagger and goes to stab the Doge but Amelia returns and rushes to place herself between Adorno and her Father.

Scene Nine. *Amelia, Gabriele and the Doge.*

AMELIA
(*sotto voce*)

Are you mad then?	Insensato!
You would kill an old man when he's sleeping?	[31] Vecchio inerme il tuo braccio colspice?

GABRIELE
(*with his voice lowered*)

I despise your attempt to defend him.	Tua difesa mio sdegno raccende.

AMELIA

But I swear that the love which unites us is pure.	Santo, il giuro, è l'amor che ci unisce,
He'll be kind to our hopes and befriend them.	Nè alle nostre speranze contende.

GABRIELE

What are you saying?	Che favelli? . . .

DOGE
(*waking*)

Ah! . . .	Ah! . . .

AMELIA

Oh, please hide your dagger.	Nascondi il pugnale,
Come. He'll hear you.	Vien . . . ch'ei t'oda . . .

GABRIELE

And fall on his mercy?	Prostrarmi al suo piede?

AMELIA

Come.	Vien.

DOGE
(*turning to Gabriele*)

I am waiting. Now kill me, you traitor!	Ecco il petto . . . colpici, sleale!

GABRIELE

Blood for blood — I, Adorno, demand it.	Sangue il sangue d'Adorno ti chiede.

DOGE

Is this true? Who has let you in by this way?	E fia ver? . . . chi t'apri queste porte?

AMELIA

I didn't.	Non io.

GABRIELE

That is a secret for ever.	Niun quest'arcano saprà.

DOGE

You will tell under torture.	Il dirai fra tormenti . . .

GABRIELE

Your tortures —   La morte,
I don't fear any torture.   Tuoi supplizi non temo.

AMELIA

Ah! forgive!   Ah pietà!

DOGE

Ah, your father has taught you your duty;	Ah! quel padre tu ben vendicasti,
He has had his revenge it is true.	Che da me contristato già fu . . .
You have stolen my treasure and beauty . . .	Un celeste tesor m'involasti . . .
She's my daughter.	La mia figlia . . .

GABRIELE

Her father — it's you!!!	Suo padre sei tu!!!
Forgive, Amelia, the jealousy,	[32] Perdon, Amelia — Indomito
The love of a cruel passion.	Geloso amor fu il mio . . .
Doge, now the veil is torn aside.	Doge, il velame squarciasi . . .
You see me now. I am a vile assassin.	Un assassin son io . . .
Put me to death then.	[33] Dammi la morte; il ciglio
I am ashamed to show you my face.	A te non oso alzar.

AMELIA

(Ah, pray look down from heaven;	(Madre, che dall'empireo
Protect me now, my mother.	Proteggi la tua figlia
Help me to beg forgiveness	Del genitor all'anima
And mercy from my father.	Meco pietà consiglia . . .
He made himself a criminal	Ei si rendea colpevole
Only through too much love.)	Solo per troppo amor.)

DOGE

(Must I forgive him — my enemy,	(Degg'io salvarlo e stendere
And give my hand in friendship?	La mano all'inimico?
Yes, let Liguria live in peace,	Si — pace splenda ai Liguri,
Placate the ancient hatreds.	Si plachi l'odio antico;
And let this be my monument;	Sia d'amistanze italiche
Write these last words on my grave.)	Il mio sepolcro altar.)

THE CROWD
(offstage; this chorus should begin a long way off, and gradually approach)

To battle now, Liguria!	[34] All'armi, all'armi, o Liguri,
Your sacred duty calls you.	Sacro dover v'appella —
The lightning of your wrath has come	Scoppiò dell'ira il folgore;
And now the night is stormy.	È notte di procella.

Let every noble Guelph surround	Le Guelfe spade cingano
The bastion of the tyrant	Di tirannia lo spalto —
And tear his palace to the ground,	Del coronato demone
And kill the fiend inside it.	Su, alla magion, l'assalto.

AMELIA
(running to the balcony)

They're shouting.   Quai gridi? . . .

GABRIELE

They are your enemies.   I tuoi nemici . . .

DOGE

I know.   Il so.

THE CROWD

Ransack and massacre!   Guerra, sterminio!

AMELIA

The crowd is gathering.

Il popolo.

S'addensa

DOGE
(to Gabriele)

Go — and join your fellows.

Va... T'unisci a' tuoi...

GABRIELE

You think I'd fight
Against you? No more.

Contro di te?... mai più.

Ch'io pugni

DOGE

Then be my herald.
Go speak to them of peace.
But let tomorrow's sun
Not rise to shine again on civil carnage.

Dunque messaggio.
Ti reca lor di pace,
E il sole di domani
Non sorga a rischiarar fraterne stragi.

GABRIELE

I shall return to your side
If what you offer does not reconcile them.

Teco a pugnar ritorno,
Se la clemenza tua non li disarmi.

DOGE
(pointing to Amelia)

Your prize will be Amelia.

Sarà costei tuo premio.

GABRIELE AND AMELIA

Oh joy beyond all hoping!

Oh inaspettata gioia!

AMELIA

Father!

O padre!

DOGE AND GABRIELE
(drawing their swords)

To battle!

All'armi!

*Renato Cioni as
Gabriele at Covent
Garden, 1965
(Houston Rogers,
Theatre Museum)*

Act Three[11]

Inside the Doge's palace. Through wide arches, Genoa can be seen illuminated for a festival; in the background the sea. / Prelude, before the curtain rises [34].

Scene One. *A Captain of the bowmen with Fiesco from the right.*

VOICES
(*offstage*)

The Doge has conquered! Evviva Simone!   Evviva il Doge! Vittoria! Vittoria!

The curtain rises.

CAPTAIN
(*giving Fiesco back his sword*)

Now you are free. Take back your weapon.   Libero sei: ecco la spada.

FIESCO

And the Guelphs?   E i Guelfi?

CAPTAIN

Defeated.   Sconfitti.

FIESCO

O sorrow to be free!   O triste libertà!

(*Enter Paolo between four guards; to Paolo:*)
What . . . Paolo?   Che? . . . Paolo?

Where are you going?   Dove sei tratto?

PAOLO
(*stopping*)

To the last of my tortures.   All'estremo supplizio.

It was my demon sent me into battle   [35] Il mio demonio mi cacciò fra l'armi
With the insurgents, and I was captured.   Dei rivoltosi e là fui colto; ed ora
Simone has
Condemned me to death. But I contrived   Mi condanna Simon; ma da me prima
To pass my own sentence first on   Fu il Boccanegra condannato a morte.
Boccanegra.

FIESCO

What is this?   Che vuoi dir?

PAOLO

He must die — I'm not afraid now —   Un velen . . . (più nulla io temo)
He must die by my poison.   Gli divora la vita.

FIESCO
(*to Paolo*)

You coward!   Infame!

PAOLO

It may be   Ei forse

Now he's already near the grave.   Già mi precede nell'avel!

---

[11] In the 1857 version, Act Three opens with a different sequence of scenes and the texts of the two versions come together again when the Doge exclaims 'Oh refrigerio!'. See page 92.

81

VOICES
(offstage)

(Look down on them from Heaven,   (Dal sommo delle sfere
Protect them both, O Lord.   Proteggili, Signor;
And may their love be given   Di pace sien foriere
The blessing of Thy word.)   Le nozze dell'amor.)

PAOLO

Oh, horror!!   Ah! orrore!!
They sing their nuptial hymn. How it   Quel canto nuzial, che mi persegue,
pursues me.
Listen. In that chapel Gabriele Adorno   L'odi? . . . in quel tempio Gabriele Adorno
Marries the girl whom I abducted . . .   Sposa colei ch'io trafugava . . .

FIESCO
(drawing his sword)

Amelia?!   Amelia?!
So it was you all along! Monster!!   Tu fosti il rapitor?! Mostro!!

PAOLO

Then kill me.   Ferisci.

FIESCO
(recovering himself)

Don't hope for that. You're promised to   Non lo sperar; sei sacro alle bipenne.
the gallows.

PAOLO
(listening to the offstage wedding chorus)

Oh horror! No more.   Orrore! Orror!

The guards take Paolo away.

Scene Two. *Fiesco alone.*

FIESCO

His words have chilled me. No, Simon, this   Inorridisco! . . . no, Simon, non questa
was not
What I had chosen. There were better   Vendetta chiesi; d'altra meta degno
ways of
Working my vengeance. Here he is. The   Era il tuo fato. — Eccolo . . . il Doge.
Doge. At last   Alfine
It is the moment for our confrontation.   È giunta l'ora di trovarci a fronte!

He withdraws into a dark corner.

Scene Three. *The Doge; he is preceded by the Captain with a trumpeter. Fiesco apart. The trumpet sounds on the balcony.*

CAPTAIN
(on the balcony, speaking to the crowd)

Men of Genoa! By the order of the Doge,   Cittadini! per ordine del Doge
Extinguish all your torches. Do not offend   S'estinguano le faci e non s'offenda
With any clamour of triumph our fallen   Col clamor del trionfo i prodi estinti.
heroes.

The Captain leaves, followed by the trumpeter. The Doge enters.

DOGE

Fire in my temples! . . . I feel a black flame, [36]   M'ardon le tempia . . . un'atra vampa sento
And it snakes through my veins . . . Oh, let   Serpeggiar per le vene . . . Ah! ch'io respiri
me breathe now,
Breathe for a moment the fresh wind of   L'aura beata del libero cielo!
heaven!

Oh, now I feel it! ... Blowing from the harbour
The salt wind, the salt wind, how it brings [37] me memories;
The thought of all those glories and those deeds of
Such renown overcomes me. How calm, how calm!
Ah, but why did I never find my death at sea then?

Oh refrigerio! ... la marina brezza!
Il mare! ... il mare! ... quale in rimirarlo
Di glorie e di sublimi rapimenti
Mi s'affaccian ricordi! Il mar! ... il mar! ...
Perchè in suo grembo non trovai la tomba? ...

FIESCO
(coming forward)

Better that way than this!

Era meglio per te!

DOGE

Who has dared come in here?

Chi osò inoltrarsi?

FIESCO

I do not fear you.

Chi te non teme ...

DOGE
(calling to the right)

Guards!

Guardie?

FIESCO

You call in vain.
Your assassins are gone.
Maybe I'll die, but first you'll hear me.

Invan le appelli ...
Non son qui sgherri tuoi.
M'ucciderai, ma pria m'odi ...

DOGE

What do you want?

Che vuoi?

The lights of the city and the port begin to go out.

FIESCO

By the festival torches that flicker, [38]
You will read of the fate that awaits you,
Where the hand of the spirit has written
Its mysterious symbols of doom.

Delle faci festanti al barlume
Cifre arcane, funebri vedrai —
Tua sentenza la mano del nume
Sovra queste pareti vergò.

The eclipse of your fortune is fated,
All your purple is hanging in tatters.
With the phantoms who hate you you'll die —
All those whom your axe denied a tomb.

Di tua stella s'eclissano i rai;
La tua porpora in brani già cade;
Vincitor tra le larve morrai
Cui la tomba tua scure negò.

The lights begin to go out in the piazza, so that none are still alight by the time the Doge dies.

DOGE

Who is speaking?

Quale accento?

FIESCO

You've heard my voice before now.

Lo udisti un'altra volta.

DOGE

Can it be? The dead come back to haunt the living?

Fia ver? — Risorgon dalle tombe i morti?

FIESCO

Or is my face so changed?

Non mi ravvisi tu?

DOGE

Fiesco!

Fiesco!

FIESCO

Simone,   Simone,
The dead have come to speak with you.   I morti ti salutano!

DOGE

Oh heaven,   Gran Dio!...
The last desire of my heart is fulfilled now.   Compito è alfin di quest'alma il desio!

FIESCO

As I appear to you   Come fantasima
Vengeance is due.   Fiesco t'appar,
Blood will have blood,   Antico oltraggio
Your days are through.   A vendicar.

DOGE

Now peace can come here   Di pace nunzio
Fiesco, through you,   Fiesco sarà...
I see an angel now   Sugella un angelo
Binding us two.   Nostra amistà.

FIESCO

Your meaning?   Che dici?

DOGE

Remember how you offered pardon ...   Un tempo il tuo perdon m'offristi ...

FIESCO

Did I?   Io?

DOGE

If I could return to you the orphan   Se a te l'orfanella concedea
Whom I thought had been lost to us for-   Che perduta per sempre allor piangea.
ever.
In Amelia Grimaldi she returned.   In Amelia Grimaldi a me fu resa,
She bears the name of her beloved mother. E il nome porta della madre estinta.

FIESCO

God! And now the truth explodes upon   Ciel!... perchè mi splende il ver sì tardi?
me?

DOGE

You're weeping. Ah, come tell why you   Tu piangi?... Perchè volgi altrove il
turn away from me.   ciglio?

FIESCO

I weep because there speaks to me   [39]   Piango, perchè mi parla
In you the voice of Heaven.   In te del ciel la voce;
I feel your love rebukes me   Sento rampogna atroce
Now with the mercy you give.   Fin nella tua pietà.

DOGE

Come, let me hold you closely,   Vien, ch'io ti stringa al petto,
The father of Maria.   O padre di Maria;
Comfort and peace enfold me   Balsamo all'alma mia
In the pardon you give.   Il tuo perdon sarà.

FIESCO

Alas, your death awaits you. You have   Ohimè! morte sovrasta ... un traditore
    been poisoned
By traitorous hands.   Il velen t'apprestò.

DOGE

Everything tells me.   Tutto favella,
I feel it ... eternity is near.   Il sento, in me d'eternità ...

84

FIESCO

Your fate is cruel!	Fato! Crudele

DOGE

She is here ...	Ella vien ...

FIESCO

Maria ...	Maria ...

DOGE

Silence, don't tell her.	Taci, non dirle ...
Just one more time I want now to bless her.	Anco una volta vo' benedirla.

He falls onto a chair.

Final Scene. *Doge, Fiesco, Maria, Gabriele, Councillors, Ladies, Gentlemen, Pages with torches, etc..*

MARIA
(*seeing Fiesco*)

There's Fiesco!	Chi veggo!

DOGE

Come ...	Vien ...

GABRIELE

(Fiesco!)	(Fiesco!)

MARIA
(*to Fiesco*)

You here!	Tu qui!

DOGE

I expect that These things surprise you. You see in Fiesco the father Of the unknown Maria who was your mother.	Deponi La meraviglia. In Fiesco il padre vedi Dell'ignota Maria, che ti die' vita.

MARIA

Fiesco? ... Can this be? ...	Egli? ... fia ver? ...

FIESCO

Maria!	Maria!

MARIA

Oh happiness! At last now the dreadful hatred's over!	Oh gioia! Allora Gli odii funesti han fine!

DOGE

Everything's finished, daughter ...	Tutto finisce, o figlia ...

MARIA

What is this cruel Thought to blight the happiest occasion?	Qual ferale Pensier t'attrista si sereni istanti?

DOGE

Maria, be brave now. Be brave and meet your sorrow.	Maria, coraggio ... A gran dolor t'appresta ...

MARIA AND GABRIELE

Oh, how fearful! What is this?	Quali accenti! oh terror!

DOGE

The final hour
Has sounded for me.

Ora suonò.   Per me l'estrema

General amazement.

MARIA AND GABRIELE

Don't say so!   Che parli?

DOGE

But the Almighty   Ma l'Eterno
Has allowed me, Maria,   In tue braccia, o Maria,
To die here in your arms.   Mi concede a spirar . . .

MARIA AND GABRIELE

What are you saying?   Possibil fia? . . .

They kneel at the Doge's feet. He rises, places his hands on their heads and, raising his eyes to heaven, says:

DOGE

Almighty Lord of Heaven,   [40] Gran Dio, li benedici
Look down on them and bless them,   Pietoso dall'empiro;
And from my life of suffering   A lor del mio martiro
Change now to flowers the thorns.   Cangia le spine in fior.

MARIA

No, do not die, the love I   No, non morrai, l'amore
Bear you will keep you from dying.   Vinca di morte il gelo;
I'll make a plea to Heaven   Risponderà dal cielo
To pity me in my sorrow.   Pietade al mio dolor.

GABRIELE

O father, O father hear me.   O padre, o padre, il seno
Fury is burning within me.   Furia mi squarcia atroce . . .
Swift are the ways of sorrow,   Come passò veloce
All of our joy now is gone.   L'ora del lieto amor!

FIESCO

All human happiness is mere   Ogni letizia in terra
Deceit and illusion.   È menzognero incanto,
An endless plain of sorrow   D'interminato pianto
Greets us when we are born.   Fonte è l'umano cor.

AMELIA AND GABRIELE

Do not die.   Non morrai.

DOGE

Come close now, my daughter, I'm dying.   T'appressa, o figlia . . . io spiro . . .
Hold me. I am dying — hold my hand in   Stringi . . . il morente . . . al cor!
  yours.

COUNCILLORS ETC.

We weep, it's true,   Sì — piange, piange, è ver,
When we are born.   Ognor la creatura;
All human nature   S'avvolge la natura
Wears a mantle forlorn.   In manto di dolor!

DOGE

Noble elders, fulfil my last request;   Senatori, sancite il voto estremo —
              (The Councillors approach.)
That the Doge's crown should grace the   Questo serto ducal la fronte cinga
  brow
Of Gabriele Adorno.   Di Gabriele Adorno.

| You, Fiesco, do what I have asked. Maria! | Tu, Fiesco, compi il mio voler . . . Maria! |

With his voice almost spent, he tries to speak and cannot. He reaches his hands out once again over his children's heads, and dies.

MARIA AND GABRIELE
(kneeling before the corpse)

| Father, father! | O padre! padre! |

FIESCO
(going to the balcony, followed by the Councillors and pages, who hold up high the burning torches)

| Men of Genoa, acclaim | Genovesi! . . . In Gabriele |
| Your latest Doge. I ask for Gabriel Adorno. | Adorno il vostro Doge or acclamate. |

VOICES
(from the piazza)

| No . . . Boccanegra! | No . . . Boccanegra! |

FIESCO

| He's dead now . . . | È morto . . . |
| Pray for the soul departed. | Pace per lui pregate! |

VOICES

| God give him peace! | Pace per lui! |

Bells toll as the curtain falls.

Kiri te Kanawa as Amelia, Robert Lloyd as Fiesco, Sherrill Milnes as Boccanegra and Veriano Luchetti as Gabriele at Covent Garden, 1980 (photo: Zoë Dominic)

Scenes from the 1857 libretto

6 The major alteration made to the 1857 score by Verdi and Boito in 1880 was the introduction of the Council Chamber scene in place of this scene. Budden (pp. 303-9) discusses various features of the original score which were 'bold' and 'novel' for the time.

Scene Ten. *A large square in Genoa.*
When the curtain rises, there is a view of the port with ships 'dressed over all'. In the distance, right, can be seen the hills with castles and palaces. Right and left, there are some magnificent buildings supported by a series of arches. These have balconies, decorated for the festivities, from which several beautifully dressed women lend their presence to the occasion. In the background, to the right, is a wide street; to the left, a broad stairway which goes up to a very fine palace. Just by the proscenium arch is a richly decorated platform. The anniversary of Boccanegra's coronation is being celebrated.

The square is crowded with people of all classes, cheerfully mingling; they carry flags, palm leaves and green branches as they sing the following chorus, until the Doge and his court arrive.

CHORUS (I)
(as they meet each other)

To the celebrations . . .	A festa!

CHORUS (II)

To the celebrations, O people of Liguria . . .	A festa, o Liguri . . .
What a beautiful day!	Splende sereno il giorno!

ALL

Already five victories won	Già cinque lustri corsero
To bring the highest glories yet	Che d'ogni gloria adorno
Since Simon was enthroned! . . .	Siede Simon sul trono! . . .

CHORUS (I)

To the celebrations! . . .	A festa! . . .

CHORUS (II)

Listen!   Udite!

ALL

Sounds   Un suono

Of rejoicing from the sea!	Di giubilo dal mar! . . .

They all go towards the seafront.

CHORUS
(off stage)

From harps, from lyres,	Sull'arpe, sulle cetere

(drawing nearer)

We draw sweet sounds . . .	Tempriam soavi accenti . . .
At the echo of so much rejoicing	L'eco di tanto giubilo
The very winds take wing.	Partin sull'ale i venti . . .

(A boat arrives with young girls in holiday dress.)

Showers of myrtle and flowers	Nembi di mirto e fiori
Among celebrating crowds	Tra festeggianti cori
Cover the land and sea.	Copran la terra e il mar.

They land and go to meet the Doge who, followed by the Senators, Paolo, Pietro and his court, emerges from the stairway to take his seat on the specially-erected platform. The people welcome him enthusiastically and the ladies wave their white handkerchiefs from the windows, throwing flowers as he passes by.

ALL

Long live Simon! . . . the love,	Viva Simon! . . . di Genova
Support and glory of Genoa;	Amor, sostegno e gloria;
You are the lightning of war,	Tu sei di guerra il fulmine,
The sun of victory!	Il sol della vittoria!
The sea shouts aloud	Delle tue gesta il grido

88

| To its furthest shores | Al più remoto lido |
| Of your deeds! | Va ripetendo il mar. |

When the Doge is seated, Prisoners and African Women appear before him, some forming into groups and others dancing their traditional dances, and sing:

MEN

| Brave warrior, here your valour | Prode guerrier, qui sfolgori |
| Blazes out in our praises. | Ne' ludi il tuo valore. |

WOMEN

| Weave, O daughter of Africa, | Intreccia, o figlia d'Africa |
| The dance of love ... | La danza dell'amore ... |

ALL

The joy of dancing in a ring	Letizia di carole
Is like the sunbeams	Agguagli i rai del sole
Which play games with the sea.	Che scherzano col mar.

The general festivities are suddenly interrupted by offstage shouts.

VOICES

| Treachery! | Tradimento! |

CHORUS

| What cries are these? ... | Quai grida! ... |

VOICES
(off stage but nearer)

| Treachery! | Tradimento! |

Scene Eleven. *As before and Gabriele who enters with an unsheathed dagger, followed by Fiesco and a few servants.*

DOGE

| Who are you, brandishing that dagger? | Chi sei tu che brandisci il pugnale? |

GABRIELE

Here I burst forth to reveal your infamy.	Qui prorompo tua infamia a scoprir.
You profit from this popular acclaim	Accoglienza tradivi ospitale,
By having your hired ruffians seize Amelia.	Festi Amelia a' tuoi sgherri rapir.

DOGE

| You are mad! | Forsennato! |

GABRIELE

| You insult me! | M'oltraggi. |

DOGE

| You lie. | Tu menti. |

GABRIELE

| You dare call Adorno a liar? | Osi Adorno nomar menzognero? |

FIESCO
(aside to Gabriele)

| (Come — put the Guelph venture to the test.) | (Vien — l'impresa de' Guelfi cimenti.) |

CHORUS
(amongst themselves)

| What mystery has suddenly arisen? | Qual si svolge improvviso mistero! |

DOGE
(quietly to Paolo)

| Where is Amelia? | Ov'è Amelia? |

89

PAOLO
(quietly to the Doge)

I don't know.

Nol so.

DOGE
(as above)

You will pay
With your life, if you do not restore her this
minute.

La tua vita
Pagherà, se lei tosto non rendi.

PAOLO
(as before)

Doge!...

Doge!...

(to Gabriele)

You, who defend this young girl,
Go... I absolve you...

Tu che la vergin difendi
Va... t'assolvo...

GABRIELE

I refuse... I'll stay here;
And I accuse you, before the Ligurian
people...
You dare to speak of pardon to me?
A pirate sits upon the throne...
Yes, he hid this chaste virgin.

Rifiuto... qui sto;
E alla Ligure gente t'accuso...
A me ardisci parlar di perdono?
Un pirata s'asside sul trono...
Si, costui vergin casta involò.

ANDREA
(quietly to Gabriele)

(Ah, you are lost!)

(Ah, sei perduto!)

GABRIELE

The Doge is wicked...

Il Doge è infame...

ANDREA
(as before to Gabriele)

Stop it.

Cessa.

DOGE

Mad!...

Folle!...

Scene Twelve. *As before and Amelia, who comes in hurriedly from the right.*

AMELIA

The Doge is innocent!

Il Doge è innocente...

ALL

Amelia!... It is she!!

Amelia... dessa!!

AMELIA
(gazing at Gabriele)

(He is safe!... O Heaven, I breathe again!
His burning love would have ruined him...
I will protect my beloved
From danger by weeping.)

(Egli è salvo!... o ciel respiro!
Lo perdea l'ardente affetto...
Dal periglio il mio diletto
Io col pianto involerò.)

DOGE
(gazing at Amelia)

(She is safe!... I breathe again!
Twice my soul lost sight
Of this lovely angel,
Twice it found her again!

(Ella è salva!... alfin respiro!
Per due volte l'alma mia
Si bell'angelo smarria,
Per due volte il ritrovò!)

GABRIELE
(gazing at Amelia)

(She is safe! At last I breathe again!   (Ella è salva! alfin respiro!
Like lightning my sword   Come fulmine il mio brando
Will fall upon the brow   Sulla fronte del nefando
Of that evil abductor.)   Rapitore piomberà.)

PAOLO AND PIETRO
(to each other)

(She is safe!... Lorenzo was   (Ella è salva!... a sue promesse
False to his promises!...   Fu Lorenzo mentitore!...
Accursed traitor,   Maledetto traditore,
He shall pay dearly for it.)   Duro fio ne pagherà.)

ANDREA AND CHORUS
(to each other)

(She is safe!... But who would dare   (Ella è salva!... ma chi osava
Ravage that virgin flower?   Oltraggiar quel vergin fiore?
Accursed be the traitor!...   Maledetto il traditore!...
The heart has no pity for him.)   Per lui taccia in cor pietà.)

*

After Amelia's account of her abduction, for which the text in both versions is the same, the scene ends thus:

CHORUS

Death to the base, Lorenzo, death!   Al vile Lorenzo la morte, la morte!

AMELIA

It is not he who, amidst so much wrong, is   Non egli è di tanto misfatto il più reo;
  the most guilty;
I, safe, promised to save his life.   Io, salva, promisi serbargli la vita.

DOGE

He may live, but exiled at once from   Ch'ei viva, ma tosto da Genova in bando.
  Genoa.

GABRIELE

Now name the villain who abducted   Or noma l'iniquo che t'ebbe rapita...
  you...

AMELIA

I'll tell the Doge...   Al Doge dirollo...

CHORUS

      To everyone...   A tutti...

DOGE

                I command   Comando,
...silence!   Tacete.

ALL

      Justice, pitiless justice,   Giustizia, giustizia tremenda,
We cry as we tremble with holy rage.   Gridiam palpitanti di sacro furor.
May the curse of Heaven and Earth fall   Del ciel, della terra l'anatema scenda
On the detested head of the vile traitor!   Sul capo esecrato del vil traditor!

There is a stage tableau and the curtain falls.

[11] This 1857 version of this act opens with a double male voice chorus, and a confused dialogue involving references to details in the original play (Budden p. 322):

Act Three

Scene as in Act Two. The awnings are pulled down over the balcony at the back. An oil-lamp burns on the table.

Scene One. *The Doge enters left followed by Gabriele, Paolo,. Pietro, Senators, Squires, Pages, etc..*

SENATORS

Doge, in your steps we see	Doge, a' tuoi passi è scorta
The bright sun of victory:	Il sol della vittoria;
A glorious new branch	Fronda di nuova gloria
To add to your gathered laurels.	Aggiungi ai colti allor.

PEOPLE
(from the piazza)

Among the turbulent clouds	Fra i procellosi nembi
Of fratricidal strife,	Delle fraterne offese,
Doge, we are inspired by you,	Doge, per te s'accese
O bright and guiding star.	Astro serenator.

DOGE

This warrior sword in my right hand gleams;	Brando guerrier nella mia destra splende;
Justice you grasp in yours.	La vostra quel della giustizia impugni.

(then to Gabriele)

Come to the church where, for your bravery,	Tu vieni al tempio, ove alla tua prodezza
Well-deserved mercy awaits you.	Degna mercè t'aspetta.

PIETRO
(aside to Paolo)

Take heart, all will be well.	Fa cor, tutto disposi.

PAOLO

At last it is time to take revenge.	Alfin l'ora suonò della vendetta.

All, except Paolo, exeunt right.

Scene Two. *Paolo, then Fiesco from the left.*

CHORUS

From your seat on high	Dal sommo delle sfere
Protect them, O Lord;	Proteggili, o Signor;
May this marriage of true love	Di pace sian foriere
Be the harbinger of peace.	Le nozze dell'amor.

PAOLO

Oh fury! . . . I have lost her now for ever! . . .	O mio furor! . . . perduta io l'ho per sempre! . . .

(He opens the door and lets Fiesco in, saying to him:)

I kept my promise — these are the Doge's Rooms . . . And your followers, who should have been with you, Where are they?	Io la promessi tenni — Ecco le stanze Del Doge . . . E i tuoi ch'esser dovean qui teco, Ove sono?

FIESCO

I do not know . . . They have fled . . .	Nol so . . . Fuggian . . .

92

PAOLO

Let us flee	Fuggiam
Too...	Noi pur...

FIESCO

Flee!...	Fuggir!...

PAOLO

If you do not want to be implicated	Se complice alla morte
In the Doge's death here plotted?	Del Doge qui segnato esser non vuoi?

FIESCO

Death!... What are you saying?...	La morte!... Che dicesti?...

PAOLO

A strong poison...	Veleno ardente...

FIESCO

Villainy!	Infame!

PAOLO

We are all	Vendicati
Revenged...	Siam tutti...

FIESCO

Terrible!... Go... Flee.	Orror!... va... fuggi.

PAOLO

And you?	E tu?

FIESCO

I shall stay here.	Qui resto.

PAOLO

I shall come back with your followers.	Io co' tuoi riederò.

Exit left.

Scene Three.

FIESCO
(alone)

Simon, I did not seek	Simon, non questa
This revenge — You were worthy	Vendetta io chiesi — D'altra fine degno
Of another end... Death will remove suspicion from me	Eri... Al sospetto di cotanta infamia
Of so much villainy...	Saprà sottrarmi morte...

He withdraws to the back.

Scene Four. *As before and the Doge, followed by Pietro from the right.*

DOGE

My brow is burning — I feel a fire	M'ardon le tempia — Un fuoco io sento
Coursing through my veins... Open the	Serpeggiar per le vene... Alle marine
Awnings to the fresh sea air.	Aure il veron dischiudi.

Pietro raises the awnings to reveal the piazza with its festive lights.

DOGE

What lights are these?	Qual fulgore?

PIETRO

The people celebrate your victory.	La tua vittoria il popolo festeggia.

Who dares disturb the peace of the dead?	Chi turbar degli estinti osa la pace?
And mocks the fallen? Go — I command you —	E schernisce ai caduti? . . . Va — comando —
This light is fading.	Questa luce s'estingua.

Exit Pietro left.

The scene continues with 'Oh refrigerio!': see page 82.

Thomas Allen as Paolo at Covent Garden, 1973 (photo: Donald Southern)

Selective Discography *by Cathy Peterson*

Conductor	E. Panizza	G. Santini	G. Gavazzeni	C. Abbado	G. Patanè
Orchestra/Opera House	Metropolitan Opera House	Rome Opera	RCA Italiana	La Scala	Hungarian State Opera
Date	1939	1957	1973	1977	1983
Simon Boccanegra	L. Tibbett	T. Gobbi	P. Cappuccilli	P. Cappuccilli	L. Miller
Fiesco	E. Pinza	B. Christoff	R. Raimondi	N. Ghiaurov	J. Gregor
Paolo	L. Warren	W. Monachesi	G. Mastromei	J. van Dam	I. Gati
Amelia	E. Rethberg	V. de los Angeles	K. Ricciarelli	M. Freni	V. Kincses
Gabriele	G. Martinelli	G. Campora	P. Domingo	J. Carreras	J. Nagy
UK Disc number	GEMM 257/8	2C163-03122/4	VLS 32627	2709 071	SLPD 12522/4
UK Tape number	–	–	VKS 32627	3371 032	MK 12522/4
US Disc number	GEMM 257/8	Seraphim 6115 *(highlights only)*	–	2709 071	SLPD 12522/4
US Tape number	–	–	–	–	MK 12522/4

The Santini recording is particularly noteworthy for the towering performances of Tito Gobbi and Boris Christoff. The best all-round version of the opera is the Deutsche Grammophon set, superbly conducted by Claudio Abbado.

The extensive extracts from the live 1938 Met. performance are of outstanding historical interest, especially for the incomparable performance of Tibbett in the title role.

For a detailed analysis of the history of *Simon Boccanegra* on records, readers are referred to Lord Harewood's article in *Opera on Record* (ed. Alan Blyth, Hutchinson, 1979).

Bibliography

The chapter devoted to *Simon Boccanegra* in *The Operas of Verdi* (Volume Two) by Julian Budden (London, 1978) is the best analysis of the opera available. It contains, inter alia, extensive quotations from the Verdi/Boito correspondence and references to the Ricordi production book published for the 1881 production at La Scala. Frank Walker (whose biography *The Man Verdi*, London, 1962, is a classic study) is the author of an article on Montanelli's contributions to the libretto in the Istituto di Studi Verdiani Bolletino, No. 3 (1960). The complete Verdi/Boito correspondence has been edited by David Rosen and Flynn Warmington for the Institute but this is not available in English.

William Weaver's *Verdi: A documentary study* (London, 1977) is a beautifully illustrated source book on the composer. *Interviews with Verdi*, collated and edited by Marcello Conati (London, 1983), gives extraordinarily vivid glimpses of the composer in the words of his contemporaries.

Readers interested in the historical background will not find any specialist accounts of Boccanegra or medieval Genoa. Apart from general studies of medieval Italian history, Daniel Waley's *The Italian City Republics* (London, 1969) and Denys Hay's *The Italian Renaissance in its Historical Background* (Cambridge, 1970) may be recommended.

Contributors

Rodolfo Celletti, a distinguished Italian musicologist, has written and lectured on many aspects of opera.

James Hepokoski is an Associate Professor of Music History at the Oberlin College Conservatory of Music. He is the author of *Giuseppe Verdi: Falstaff* in the Cambridge Opera Handbook series. He is currently preparing a similar volume on *Otello* and has written articles on Verdi and Debussy.

Desmond Shawe-Taylor, music critic of *The New Statesman & Nation* (1945-1958) and subsequently of *The Sunday Times*, has contributed about 75 entries on famous singers to *The New Grove*.